Brian Kelly
for the
United States Senate
from PA

Pennsylvania needs a fresh face that loves America more than politics.

The political game is rigged. You need way too much money to win. I have only enough money to live so I decided to run for US Senator as a JFK-like Democrat against Robert P Casey Jr.—as a write-in candidate. My plan is to spend as little as possible on my campaign. Therefore, I will have to find every means possible without spending money to be able to point out the issues I hope to solve and the specific platform to bring home those solutions.

I am not a fool, but most would say my quest is a fool's errand. Try running for office in a state such as Pennsylvania, in which the political incumbents and the establishment have the game 100% rigged. Corrupt state politicians in all 50 states have slanted the ballot-access table in favor of incumbents and against non-political regular citizens of America such as me and you when you become inclined to throw your hat in the ring. If not us, then who—a politician and we just cannot have that.

Using this experience as a basis, this book is written to help all potential candidates understand the reality of restrictive ballot access laws in all the states and what one must do to comply with them and/or get around them. For me, this book will describe my unique platform for Pennsylvania and America in detail. For you, if you ever choose to run for office, it will serve as an effective learning tool and a how-to guide. It contains a lot of great platform information, a great announcement speech, and helpful stuff that you can use in your campaign.

If you were planning to vote Democrat, please vote for me instead of Bob Casey Jr. I will serve you better for sure. I do like Lou Barletta and he is a very good choice in the event I am not elected this time out.

My platform as shown in this book and on the web-site will be the major vehicle that I use to present my ideas to the American people, especially Pennsylvanians. Besides being a 100% advocate for the Trump agenda, the following points make my candidacy special & unique:

1. Two solutions for resident illegal foreign nationals who today live in the shadows.
2. Proposal with justification to Boost Social Security Now!
3. Proposal with justification to Wipe Out All Student Debt Now!

You won't want to put this book down as you learn the specifics of my platform as well as the ins & outs of running for office and the rudiments of running a campaign. Moreover, you will learn how Brian Kelly ran for Congress in 2010 and Mayor in 2015. Kelly has yet to win but think about Robert the Bruce (spider) and *the little engine that could,* and you will know what motivates your author.

ii

Published by: .... LETS GO PUBLISH!
Editor in Chief..Brian P. Kelly
Email: .... info@letsgopublish.com
Web site..www.letsgopublish.com

Library of Congress Copyright Information Pending
Book Cover Design by **Katie Kelly & Pat Kelly**

Text Editor—Brian P. Kelly

ISBN Information: The International Standard Book Number (ISBN) is a unique machine-readable identification number, which marks any book unmistakably. The ISBN is the clear standard in the book industry. 159 countries and territories are officially ISBN members. The Official ISBN for this book is

978-1-947402-48-5

The price for this work is:... **$ 7.95 USD**

10	9	8	7	6	5	4	3	2	1

Release Date: ....August 2018

Dedication

I dedicate this book to my wonderful wife Patricia; our three wonderful children Brian, Mike and Katie; and our friendly friends—Ben our always very happy dog, who recently became an Angel, and Buddy, our always cheerful Catholic cat.

Thank You All!

Acknowledgments

I appreciate all the help that I have received in putting this book together as well as all of my other 164 other published books.

My printed acknowledgments had become so large that book readers "complained" about going through too many pages to get to page one of the text.

And, so to permit me more flexibility, I put my acknowledgment list online, and it continues to grow. Believe it or not, it once cost about a dollar more to print each book.

Thank you and God bless you all for your help.

Please check out www.letsgopublish.com to read the latest version of my heartfelt acknowledgments updated for this book. FYI, Wily Ky Eyely, my wonderful basketball playing "niece," loves this book and recommends it to all. She wants "Uncle Brian" to be our next US Senator.

Click the bottom of the Main menu to see the big acknowledgments!

Thank you all!

Preface

Why did Brian W. Kelly write this book?

Brian W. Kelly loves America and he developed a number of unique approaches to solving some problems in America, from which Pennsylvanians suffer about as much as those from other states.

Kelly has written a number of books on immigration for example. Each one further defines the problem and refines the solution. Kelly's solution revealed in his platform for Americans solves the problem once and for all of upwards of 60 million illegal foreign residents living in the shadows.

Brian wrote this book among other reasons because he cares about Pennsylvania and America. I am publishing this book because I care. This book identifies a number of unique solutions for seniors, millennials, and the rest of us. When elected as your Senator Brian W. Kelly will work hard to assure these notions become reality. You'll ask yourself why nobody else thought of that when you finish reading Brian's platform points.

I hope you enjoy this book and I hope that it inspires you to take the individual actions necessary to help the government of the US stand firm against any attacks on democracy from outside or from within this great country.

A great start of course is to stop the Congress's gouging of our senior Americans and our young adult Americans. As you know seniors are plagued with massive government sanctioned inflationary reductions in Social Security payments whereas young Americans are literally in a debtor's prison as it is impossible to escape the burden of 1.48 trillion dollars of student debt.

As Americans know, this keeps the most physically capable generation of young adults on the sidelines rather than being able to participate in American life. Brian Kelly has the solutions to help a fellow Senators and a willing Congress to solve this deep moral dilemma for our country.

I wish you the best.

Brian P. Kelly, Publisher
Wilkes-Barre, Pennsylvania

Table of Contents

About the Author

Brian W. Kelly retired as an Assistant Professor in the Business Information Technology (BIT) program at Marywood University, where he also served as the IBM i and Midrange Systems Technical Advisor to the IT Faculty. Kelly designed, developed, and taught many college and professional courses. He continues as a contributing technical editor to a number of IT industry magazines, including "The Four Hundred" and "Four Hundred Guru," published by IT Jungle.

Kelly is a former IBM Senior Systems Engineer and IBM Mid Atlantic Area Specialist. His specialty was designing applications for customers as well as implementing advanced IBM operating systems and software facilities on their machines.

He has an active information technology consultancy. He is the author of 165 books and numerous technical articles. Kelly has been a frequent speaker at COMMON, IBM conferences, and other technical conferences.

Brian was a candidate for US Congress from Pennsylvania in 2010 and he brings a lot of experience to his writing endeavors and he is ready to be your Senator in 2019.

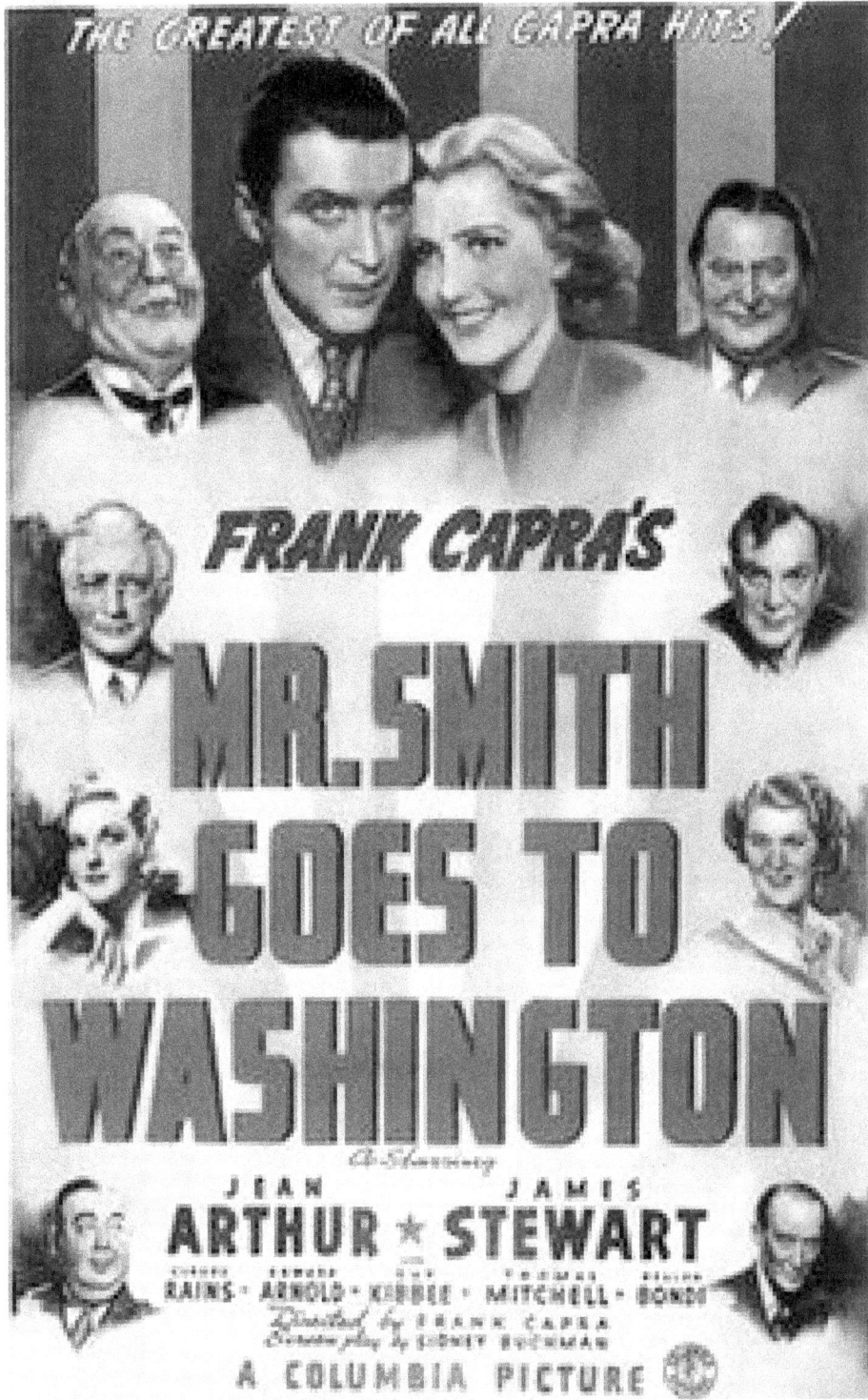

Chapter 1 Unique Characteristics of Brian Kelly's US Senate Platform

Note from your author and Senate Candidate Brian W. Kelly

Brian Kelly Chief Technology Officer College Misericordia in 1994

No, I don't look like this anymore, but I did look like this when as the chief technology officer at College Misericordia in the 1990's, I began to pay a lot more attention to what goes on in our government. The College paid for this picture.

By now, I admit that I am not too happy with what I discovered about government and politics in our country. That, and because like you, I could not afford a full-bore Senatorial campaign, is why I am running as a write-in candidate for the US Senate.

Ask yourself this question: Would you hire any Congressman in America today to run your business—even to babysit your kids? Me neither! Yet, we hire them through the electoral process to run the most complex country that ever was—the United States of America. It is clear that at some point we must begin to make better choices. Why not start in 2018?

I think the best way to begin this book is to give you the announcement speech that I was ready to give the first time I would be given a forum in a cost-free venue. There is a lot in this speech but then again, there are many issues today in America. As I review the contents of this speech below, I wish that I could make the speech shorter and at the same time more comprehensive, so you fully know what the platform is all about and why it is worthy of your consideration. I have done my best, but I do admit that this is not one of my shortest speeches. Thank you.

Originally, I wrote this speech for Congressman Lou Barletta, hoping he would adopt the platform elements in this speech as his own. I believe the Congressman likes these ideas but as he is running for Senator as a Republican, it would be difficult to convincing officials in the Republican Party of their worth. It would be tough to push a platform that may have a negative effect on the budget cuts Republicans are seeking. And, so, I decided to go it alone, and instead of expecting the man who I believe may still become Senator Barletta present these ideas for America, I will do the job myself under my own write-in candidacy.

Yet, please, if you must vote Democrat in this election, remember that unlike Bob Casey Jr., I am not a Chuck Schumer or Nancy Pelosi Democrat nor am I a Maxine Watters Democrat nor do I stand for any principle such as the abolishment of ICE that harms the country I love.

I would be pleased to accept your vote of confidence for my candidacy. Just write me in.

B-R-I-A-N K-E-L-L-Y

Don't type the dashes.

Campaign Update August 3, 2018

This is the day after the Donald Trump Rally in Wilkes-Barre, my home town, on behalf of Republican Lou Barletta for the US Senate. As a result of that 1 hour and sixteen-minute rally, Donald Trump's phenomenal speech, his endorsement of Lou Barletta, and an equally great and inspiring speech by Senate Candidate Lou Barletta, I have decided to endorse Congressman Lou Barletta for the US Senate. I am as much **opposed** to Senator Robert 'Sleepin Bob' Casey as I am **in favor** of a great American, Lou Barletta, a man who shares most of my values.

For those Democrats who historically will not vote for a Republican under any circumstances, or those Democrats desiring the package of unique pro-American legislation that I have developed in the past, I encourage you to make a better choice for the US Senate than Bob Casey. Pennsylvania needs a great US Senator. Casey has not been that man and his concern for the people is getting worse, not better. Lou Barletta is the best choice. However, if you must vote Democrat, remember that Bob Casey is not for the people of Pennsylvania. Rather than vote for Casey, you may feel free to write my name in for United States Senator B-R-I-A-N K-E-L-L-Y. I am a registered Democrat. Thank you.

At the PA Wilkes-Barre Rally, President Trump and Congressman Barletta netted out the same negative case against Bob Casey, Jr as a legislator. Trump began by saying the younger Casey was boring, a nobody in Washington who does what Democratic leaders tell him. I don't think I ever met him, Trump said. Bob Casey is for open borders, Trump asserted, again raising the specter of violent immigrants from Central America overrunning the country.

Barletta and Trump noted that Casey is a pro-abortion, anti-second amendment socialist by his record and he expects Casey to be calling for the abolition of the Immigration and Customs Enforcement (ICE) agency, a favorite cause on the left. He more or less said that Chuck Schumer says "Jump," and Bob Casey says: "How high?" Then, every, time, he goes ahead and jumps. Though Casey says he is not anti-ICE, he also says he is anti-abortion and then votes pro-abortion in almost all cases, such as his opposition to Judges Gorsich and Cavanaugh. For twelve years, Bob Casey Jr. has been the epitome of a do-nothing politician, choosing not to do the people's business. It is time for Casey to make a graceful exit.

Like me, Lou Barletta is for the entire Trump agenda, especially the Wall, and that will be good for America. The only thing that we disagree on is a detailed solution that I put together in several books this year that squarely address resident illegal foreign nationals, Fair COLAs for Seniors, and a major economic stimulus by solving the student loan crisis.

End of Campaign Update

God bless you all and I hope you enjoy my speech. It is so right on for today that I enjoy it every time I read or edit it. Here it is:

Fellow Citizens,

Language is inadequate to express my gratitude for the privilege of submitting before you my candidacy to represent the fine people of Pennsylvania as your US Senator.

I would also like to thank you for the fine welcome, which you all have extended to me on this occasion. As I look out in my mind's eye, I see a vast sea of human faces who share a common interest, as do I, about the greatest questions of our times. Beyond occasionally agitating the mind, they now dominate the concerns of all Pennsylvanians and U.S. citizens, underlying the foundations of our free institutions. Let us all make sure that freedom never becomes just another word for nothing left to lose.

The reaction of my U.S. Senate candidacy by the people of Pennsylvania has been quite heartening. We have a president whose interest quite simply is to "Make America Great Again." By contrast, the embedded establishment and liberal leftovers in the SWAMP, have no interest in performing what is good for our country. They are doing their best to undermine our president, without any repercussions, aided and abetted by a corrupt media, instead of building bridges to work for the good of all Americans.

It is no longer acceptable for a Democrat or a Republican to be a Never-Trumper. Donald Trump is our president and his platform is my platform and when elected, I hope the extras in my platform that I introduce in this speech, become part of the Trump platform.

We all know that "Never-Trumpers" will never hold office again. Democrats such as Bob Casey Jr., my opponent, simply adore the establishment's impediments to the president's agenda with a media whose interests are as adverse to the American people as the British press was during Colonial Times.

The Democrats and the Republican Never-Trumpers in the Senate, House, and the federal bureaucracy and the degenerate mainstream press have done everything they can to thwart the will of 62,979,636 people who voted to clean out the SWAMP with a fresh new presidential administration.

The legendarily venal Hillary Clinton lost the election after the public saw through her charade; yet she continues to parade around the world blaming everything from her own adoring fans at The New York Times, to white women like her, to the DNC, and probably even the cows in Wisconsin, a state she famously lost after taking it so for granted, she never visited.

She even blames the FBI and it never occurs to anyone that the best way to avoid an untimely FBI intervention in a political campaign is to *not run for President while under federal criminal investigation*. And all the while, Senator Casey stood by submissively, applauding and enabling this farce of a candidacy. It is time for the country to move on. She lost, now get over it. We've had twelve years of Casey and that's about as much as any man or woman in America can stand.

I am running for the US Senate to reclaim this seat which rightfully belongs to its people, not the extrinsic interests controlling our politicians who would tear the Constitution in half without hesitation if it would please their donors and cheerleaders in the mainstream media. Despite the shameless lack of virtue that defines the top echelons of our government, our country itself is replete with honest citizens who would be humbled to work on behalf of their fellow countrymen and women. That is why I am running for the US Senate against one of the biggest icons of mainstream mediocrity and corruption, Mr. Bob Casey Jr.

Casey Jr. caters only to the whining anti-Trump crowd who wants to turn every trivial post on Facebook into a new Cuban Missile Crisis. Despite the voters in even his home state rejecting the rank duplicity of former Secretary Clinton and her bleak vision of hopelessness and sovereign state decline, Senator Casey never lifted a finger to help the people who support our president, despite the fact that we outnumber the opposition right here in Pennsylvania. But to him-- that's Bob Casey, folks; we do not even exist.

The Bob Casey Jr. that we all see is a do-nothing Senator who would prefer to turn the US into a globalist abyss rather than support its sovereignty or its people's dignity. Meanwhile, our great president is trying to find everybody a high-paying job by making it easier to conduct business in our country. I intend to help President Trump protect us from such parasitic interests.

If there is one principle most cherished in all free governments, it is that which asserts the exclusive right of a free people to form and adopt their own fundamental laws, to manage and regulate their own internal affairs and domestic institutions. That is under constant attack by Mr. Casey and his legions of Clinton dead-enders.

Electing representatives of the people is not a triviality, but rather the expression of the most fundamental right of self-government. Without it, of course, this great United States would be like any other country in the world. It would not be the exceptional republic, which we the people have enjoyed since our own Declaration of Independence.

To say that I am honored to be here today presenting my candidacy for the US Senate, would be the understatement of the ages. Thank you for your reception and hospitality. I assure you that if elected, I will provide Pennsylvania and the United States of America the best representation in the US Senate of which I am capable. You can be sure of that.

We have many issues today of which the people are concerned. My plan in this address is to limit discussion to just four of the most prominent. My candidacy uniquely addresses each of the four as no other candidate for any US office has ever been able to do. I hope you will find the elements of my platform a welcome refreshment and inclusive of precepts that we all embrace and recognize as sincere and necessary.

My format will be to be present each issue by area of concern and then offer the specific solution which is part of my unique platform. The issues and solutions will be presented one by one in the following four topical areas:

#1—Obamacare.

#2—Illegal Immigration.

#3—Student Debt Crisis Wipe Out All Student Debt Now!

#4—Social Security's Cost-of-Living Fraud – Boost
          Social Security Now!

My pledge is to put forth legislation when elected to help address all four issues. Let's discuss them one by one, starting with Obamacare.

Obamacare

The first problem on the list is #1 because over 54% of Americans say that the availability and affordability of healthcare is their #1 issue. Despite Obama's empty promises, many of us cannot keep our favorite doctors nor can we retain an affordable health plan that meets our needs. The costs have been so prohibitive that many Americans have forestalled doctor's visits with often grave consequences. We all know that despite what Bob Casey would offer you, Obamacare is a disaster.

My solution to Obamacare begins with clarity and definitive purpose. We start with a one-line repeal. The beast is vanquished. Following the repeal, we envision a plethora of competing less expensive alternatives provided by the marketplace without current tyrannical government controls.

Illegal Immigration

In February 2004, Arizona Senator John McCain recognized via Border Patrol reports that nearly four million people crossed our borders "illegally" each year following the Reagan amnesty in 1986. Nonetheless, the fraudulent press insists that the total count of illegal immigrants residing in the United States is eleven million, a mathematical impossibility if Border Patrol figures are to be believed. And of these millions of foreigners, countless amounts receive welfare while, contrary to popular mythology, very few actually work in agriculture.

There may be as many as 60 million and perhaps more illegal foreign nationals living in the United States today. While some individuals in this group may contribute to our society, on balance this is outweighed by the group's overall negative effect on our resources, whether they be drained by government assistance, lost employment opportunities for American citizens, or criminal offenses. It is amazing how effective the fake-ID business is in turning illegal aliens into fake citizens who are thus enabled to enjoy American rights and privileges.

According to the 2011 GAO report entitled "Criminal Alien Statistics," the cost of crimes by illegal foreign nationals is $8.1 billion per year, and that's without even considering the incomprehensibly larger emotional toll this takes on families whose priceless loved ones can never be replaced.

If elected, I will introduce two pieces of legislation that will solve this problem of illegal residents in the shadows once and for all. Besides many other benefits, it stands to save the U.S. over $1 Trillion per year in addition to major reductions in crime. The two solutions are known as pay-to-go and the resident visa program.

Pay-to-Go

It costs taxpayers $30,000 per year on the average, per illegal alien in America. Each illegal resident and their dependent children, who signs up for Pay to Go, on the way back to the home country, will receive a one-time $20,000 stipend plus the individual expense back to the home country. With a cost of $30,000 per year to support unwelcome interlopers, the taxpayer savings begins year one and continues at $30,000 per year forever. Not a bad deal for Americans.

The program therefore quietly accommodates family reunification in the home country. A family of five for example, could do quite well back home after receiving $100,000 in stipends from Uncle Sam. Reuniting families in their own countries is a good idea for them and for America. The savings in welfare means there is no cost in year one and in year 2, the savings equal $30,000 for each person who "goes." back home, never to return.

Resident Visa

Those who do not want to leave the US can sign up, be vetted, and eventually be approved for the Resident Visa. The visa will cost $200.00 to cover vetting in year one and it will be renewable every year thereafter for $100.00 To get a Resident Visa, a former interloper would agree to all stipulations after registering. Stipulations would include full initial vetting; onsite renewal vetting; keep existing jobs; new jobs for Americans first; no voting; no citizenship; no welfare and no freebies of any kind. Everybody is not automatically approved.

After vetting, those not approved for the resident visa program may use the Pay-to-Go program to aid in their relocation.

As the program would entail 100% participation from illegal residents, estimates are as high as $500 billion per year cost savings in total for those who choose to go or for those who choose to stay using the no-welfare resident visa. Another $500 billion will be reclaimed over time for lost wages. Additionally, if we can figure a way for countries to reclaim their criminals, there is another $8.1 billion to be recovered.

Once the program is in effect, there would be no more illegal aliens in the country. Resident Visa holders would be legal and so there would be no shadows. There would be no need for DACA and no need for Sanctuary cities Let me repeat that. All issues with DACA would be over and Sanctuary Cities would be a thing of the past because there would be no shadows and no illegal interlopers.

Two additional programs are the part of my platform that I would now like to introduce. Like the resident alien plans, no other candidate for public office includes these great programs in their platform. You are going to love these.

These two new programs offer the promise of a positive effect on the health of the economy and both will contribute to improving it for American citizens of all ages to live well in this country. The first is about wiping out all student debt and the second is about offering Social Security recipients increased benefits to make up for fraudulent cost of living increases based on an intentionally fraudulent consumer price index.

Student Debt is Huge

If we look at the $1.48 Trillion dollars in student loan debt that more and more young adults simply cannot repay, some have asked: "Why do our young people no longer matter?" Do they matter?

We live in an age when everybody seems to have a reason to pick on millennials. They would not loan a "spoiled" millennial "ingrate" as much as a dollar for a cup of coffee.

Whether millennials are deserving of the bad rap or not, they represent a lost generation of our society. For the sake of all of America, they need to be invited back in. We all have student loan debtors in our families – sons, daughters, nephews, nieces, even grandparents and parents when we consider cosigners.

I plan to offer legislation when first elected to make sure we solve this nasty American problem. There have been many other debt reliefs in our history but none that could deliver such an immediate benefit to so many actual Americans all at once. The upside would be overwhelming, a joint humanitarian return and a major economic return far greater than any bailout in history. Let's consider that .

A Bailout is a Bailout?

Many of us remember bailouts of the past from 2007 onward. We had bank bailouts, auto company bailouts, TARP bailouts and many other unnamed bailouts. Did any of these help your family? Of course not. Bailout fever began right before Obama became President and continued. The President managed all of the money—trillions. He chose not to give a dime to help student loan debt but spared no expense showering the degenerate financial institutions that owned his candidacy with gold.

Mike Collins, a Forbes Magazine contributor whose expertise focuses on manufacturing and government policy (not the former beloved magistrate of Wilkes-Barre who shares the same name) had this to say:

"Most people think that the big bank bailout was the $700 billion that the treasury department used to save the banks during the financial crash in September of 2008. But this is a long way from the truth because the bailout [ten years later] is still ongoing.

The Special Inspector General for TARP's summary of the bailout says that the total commitment of government is $16.8 trillion dollars with the $4.6 trillion already paid out. The [same] banks are now larger and still too big to fail. But it isn't just the government bailout money that tells the story of the bailout. This is a story about lies, cheating, and a multi-faceted corruption, which was often criminal."

Like most elements of his presidency, Obama made the situation worse when he commandeered the student loans from Sallie Mae and other lenders. The government now pulls in more than $50 billion a year from charging high interest rates to student borrowers. The Obama Student Loan Company charged 6.8% as a student interest rates. The CBO estimates that the interest rate on these loans could quickly be reduced from 6.8 percent to 5.3 percent if Obama had not earmarked the profit from the backs of students to subsidize Obamacare.

Not only were millennials duped into huge college loans when they were so young that Clearasil was one of their major expenses, they were duped into believing Obama was in their corner.

I believe these student victims deserve a break. They are now adults. Some stuck with huge cosign tabs are grandparents on Social security. The government actually garnishes their SSR to pay back the Obama loans.

The federal government is putting up $16.8 trillion dollars as of 2018 to big banks, and other nameless faces receiving bailouts. We still do not know who is getting our money. Yet students who are still being victimized by usury were preyed on as 17-year- olds by admissions counsellors for an all-but worthless college education leading to no job. If given the choice would you be helping the big banks or our own kids?

What do the people think about Student Debt?

Four in ten Americans believe that President Trump's administration should forgive all federal student debt in order to help stimulate the economy, according to a reasonably new survey revealed in 2017. As time goes by as more Americans realize we are excluding a full generation of Americans in our economy, this number will increase from a simple majority to an overwhelming endorsement of wiping out this scurrilous unfair debt as soon as possible. We should bring these

48 million students back into the American way of life as soon as possible.

The largest share blame for the student debt crisis lies with the promises made by over-zealous admissions counsellors convincing kids to sign up for $100,000 loans. No American can want a full generation of other Americans to be left behind in the Trump economy. We need this debt eradicated now and to install safeguards so that seventeen-year-olds in the future are never asked again to sign up for a life in debtor's prison.

According to MoneyTips.com, attitudes have changed from a time when Americans thought college students should be punished for making bad choices to today, when we could use 48 million new spenders in our economy. They would be unleashed into a world of productivity if no longer burdened with massive debt. Many of us know first-hand the consequences of this debt burden. Though millennials may not be the most gracious in asking for help, they are Americans, not DACA immigrants, and they need our help now.

The raw economic fact regardless of your philosophical preference is that spenders with the greatest potential to spend today are not spending at all in real numbers because of student debt. They are not getting married. They are not having families and they are not buying homes. We must solve this scourge on our country so that this generation can produce other generations of Americans.

Our children are not MS-13 members in disguise; there are our kids. American kids. They were snookered to join academia for what they were deceived into believing was an indispensable college degree by depraved loan sharks. Let's give them a full chance. It costs a university nothing when their students with huge loans fail. Please let that sink in.

Let me review the plight of young American college attendees and graduates. Barely out of adolescence, these young Americans were wheedled into commitments based on fraudulent promises by admissions counselors and financial institutions. It was unfair to pit experienced loan sharks against adolescent teenagers. The students were further damned by a paid-for Congress, whose lobbyists insisted that these select few with student debt, distinct from all of the others in America, had no opportunity for any relief in the bankruptcy courts.

Non-college graduates with a trillion dollars in credit card debt are still able to obtain full relief from the courts. Why did Congress exclude these former teenagers, who clearly have been the biggest victims of loan-sharking organized racketeering ever seen in America? Why?

I am pledging today to solve this problem as soon as I can. I am ready to take action. I hope you all agree. Let's help these young Americans before they are lost forever.

Young teenagers were told all through high school that the best ticket for a successful life is a college education. Is this true today? Their salaries often lag behind even those of non-college educated professionals such as plumbers, electricians, computer repair personnel, operating engineers, and more. Because of their reliance on these deliberately false misrepresentations, they now owe an approximate average of $50,000 in student debt while their admissions counsellors and loan sharks revel in riches, in their Mercedes, BMW's, and third vacation home on the lake.

Unscrupulous malefactors with self-interested agendas persuaded America's teenagers, many so young they still had Acne vulgaris, to dig themselves huge financial holes with no escape. Universities are at least partly responsible for their unfulfilled promises. Don't you think? We must also consider what liability they may share in compensating this lost generation where one out of six student borrowers must default today, a figure that only increases with time.

Removing this debt may not fully compensate for the bad hand they were dealt, but its consequent increase in economic activity will benefit all of us. It will boost the US economy beyond expectations. We are already giving bailouts of $17 billion to obscenely rich people in corporate shadows. Right now, we need a mere 10% of that to pay for the write-off of student debt without hurting taxpayers and without putting any banks under. The savings over three years, for example from the resident visa program alone pays off all the student debt that exists today. Why support illegal aliens when we can help Americans?

One last point. It helps to recall that President Obama increased the National Debt by $9.1 Trillion in just eight years, hoping to assure that illegal aliens had all the resources they needed to take as many American jobs as they could. This is six times the amount of debt owed by young Americans. Obama nearly doubled our debt. And what do we have to show for that? As is typical for the Obama years, the answer is frankly... nothing. By contrast, debt relief for our young Americans will be *visibly* positive in its impact.

So, let's say Congress wipes out all student debt because it is the fair thing to do. How do we prevent this from every happening again? For this, I thank my great friend, Dennis Grimes whose solution combines some skin in the game for Academic Institutions to the mix and thus assures that no student will ever carry debt unless the student is successful with a job in their field of study. Here is how the new loan system would work.

Nobody gets a loan unless the college or university agrees to take all of the risk of the loan. If the student is successful, she or he will pay reasonable amounts on a monthly basis. If the student is jobless, since the university vouched for the student, the school will owe all of the debt. Academic institutions are smart. They will stop lending quickly to students with very little prospects of being able to pay the loan back. If students do not maintain acceptable averages, they will be expelled, and the university will pay their balance. If they want to go to college in the future, it will be cash only. What do you think?

A Rigged System

I am confident that President Trump would re-enfranchising America's youngest generation of adults by eradicating student debt and pay the balance via savings no longer spent subsidizing illegal immigrants.

In his own words, regarding recent graduates: "They go, and they work, and they take loans, and they're borrowed up, and they can't breathe, and they get through college and the worst thing is, they go through that whole process and they don't have any job." Trump has it right. He sees how this rigged system has snuffed out the optimism of a bright generation that now gives way to cynicism and despair.

If I am elected as your Senator, I will help enact legislation that eradicates all Student Debt, effective immediately.

Boost Social Security Now

Social Security is no longer publicly discussed by our duplicitous media despite the fact that seniors' issues need the spotlight now more than ever. The media derided the implied greed of SSR recipients who received a whopping two percent cost of living raise to kick off 2018, as if oblivious to the fact that the inflation rate for 2017 was nearly 11%. Not 2%, but 11%.

No wonder seniors are struggling when their cost for purchases goes up 11% and their COLA to make up for that is a mere 2%. How do I know that, and you don't?

There are several ways Americans can investigate how much government lies cost them each year. The government purposely underestimates the cost of living to deprive our elderly of a commensurate actual increase in earned benefits. One such method for you to use is to subscribe to the Chapwood index or you may explore Shadowstats.com.

Seniors unfortunately are running out of whatever financial cushions they may ever have had, and their plight today is dire. I encourage you all to research the degree to which government deceptions are resulting in these surreptitious deprivations.

After decades being saturated by our mainstream propaganda rags, it is refreshing to finally see the truth in print. The Chapwood Index reflects the true cost-of-living increase in America. It is updated and released twice a year. There the ruses or mis-directions of the government are not included in its pages. Instead, it truthfully reports the unadjusted actual cost and price fluctuation of the top 500 items on which Americans spend their after-tax dollars in the 50 largest cities in the nation.

It exposes why middle-class Americans—salaried workers who are given routine pay hikes and retirees who depend on annual increases in their corporate pension and Social Security payments—cannot maintain their standard of living. Plainly and simply, the Index shows that their income can't keep up with their expenses and it explains why they increasingly have to turn to the government for entitlements for supplementation.

Mainstream Democrats like Senator Casey and Nancy Pelosi exacerbate the situation by allowing use of even more inequitable methods such as the new chained CPI to help assure that Seniors can languish in poverty as soon as possible.

The problem of lacking transparency on true costs (true inflation) occurs because salary and benefit increases are pegged to the fraudulent Consumer Price Index (CPI), which for more than a century has purported to reflect the fluctuation in prices for a typical "basket of goods" in American cities — but which actually hasn't done that for more than 30 years

The middle class has seen its purchasing power decline dramatically in the last three decades, forcing more and more people to seek entitlements when their savings are gone. And as long as pay raises and benefit increases are tied to a false CPI, this trend will continue.

In the past, nobody was anxious to throw the proverbial grandma under the bus. Now, believe it or not, hordes of constituencies are lining up to be the first to fleece what should belong to her into the eternal abyss, never to be seen again. The list of offenders includes: Congress, government officials, professors in academia, the "greatest" economic advisors the world has ever known, and dejected stand-alone economists who failed to gain tenure at a university.

This group of elite misfits have formed a diabolical consortium to cheat seniors out of their due cost of living increases promised from the very day the SSR act was passed by Franklin Delano Roosevelt.

As the mainstream Democrats kowtow to cultural elites and financial institutions, turning their backs on the workers and middle-class that defined their constituency for much of the 20th century, it is up to us to pick up the slack and fight for the rights of everyday Americans. When SSR was enacted, the president promised full dollar value throughout the years in order to ensure its passage in 1933. We cannot let this be undermined by the likes of Senator Casey and his allies under Chuck Schumer and Nancy Pelosi.

Many Americans are concerned that the Social Security program itself may not be able to sustain itself while others see the government cheating on the cost of living increases (CPI) thereby predetermining a life of squalor for seniors.

All successful societies throughout the ages, have maintained respect and dignity for their elders. Not only is cheating seniors a moral failure, it is a sign of a civilization entering an era of decay.

While seniors are losing their homes and many, for want of bread and milk, are on the verge of heading to the proverbial poorhouse or worse—the clutches of the Grim Reaper, Congress in 2018 pretended to care, giving a 2% raise, but then quickly snatched it right back in the dead of night via a Medicare Part B premium increase. This additional Medicare Part B charge for necessary health services for seniors was excluded from the cost of living calculations.

Thus, to pay Medicare part B, seniors are forced to use their "generous" 2% raises there, rather than to offset the costs brought forth from inflation in 2017 for which the 2% was intended. Since the real inflationary cost increases were closer to 11%, that means that instead of 9% that seniors were to endure, they accrued a full load of 11% in price increases. It's easy to understand why this constant drainage of resources is unsustainable for a senior citizen.

How did we reach this point?

Early in the administration of disgraced former President Bill Clinton, an economist named Michael Boskin, and Alan Greenspan, Chairman of the Board of Governors of the Federal Reserve System, devised a scheme that would allow for market basket "substitutions" to artificially lower the cost of living and result in lower payments to our oldest Americans. Prior to their involvement, the consumer price index (CPI) was measured using the cost of a fixed basket of goods, a fairly simple and straightforward concept.

The identical basket of goods would be priced at prevailing market costs for each period, and the period-to-period change in the cost of that market basket represented the rate of inflation in terms of maintaining a constant standard of living. That was self-evidently fair and reasonable, and predictably resulted in seniors receiving annual COLA increases in tandem with the prices of goods actually increasing.

But Boskin and Alan Greenspan argued that when one item in the basket, for instance steak, became too expensive, the consumer would substitute hamburger for the steak, and that the inflation measure should reflect the costs tied to buying hamburger rather than the steak. Eventually, it became OK for the bureaucrats to replace hamburger with less expensive tuna and eventually because the protein value was the same, cat tuna replaced regular tuna in the market basket.

To further obscure the true cost of living, other items were selectively removed from the basket when the prices were high and then reinserted when the prices were low.

Many people have been familiar with this ruse. For example, a 1970s economic commentator named Barry Ritholtz joked that Greenspan's core inflation metric can more accurately be described as "inflation ex-inflation," meaning inflation after all of the inflation has been excluded. This demonstrates that the deception of seniors has been intentional, and it continues with a new notion called the chained CPI that will cost seniors even more.

The fact is that government has deceitfully stolen right from the pockets of our beloved seniors by denying them a fair cost of living increase. Some have even suggested that the government believes a natural limit exists on the criticism this could engender because over time, many of the complaints will be silenced by their deaths. Charming.

Walter J. Williams, an American blessing who operates the Shadowstats site has demonstrated that seniors have been stiffed by much more than just 125% and in fact should be receiving more than 4 times what their dollars were worth in 1980. That's $450 instead of $100.00. Any senior would love to have even a small proportion of that loss back.

I hope I have convinced you all that seniors have been ripped off and are being ripped off financially by their government. Congress is the real culprit.

So, what do I recommend for now? A gradual remedy. Since it would be difficult to give seniors the proper increase immediately needed to offset this quagmire caused by government malfeasance, my recommendation would be to approach it gradually, in a way that seniors would be somewhat pleased, and be able to live out their golden years in a more dignified manner.

For the next four years, the COLA boost that I'd recommend would be 15% above the real inflation rate. After four consecutive years, that should be sufficient to remove seniors from the on-deck circle they currently occupy directly outside the homeless shelter. That's all it would take.

Thank you for your attention on these important matters.

In conclusion, I must again express my gratitude for your consideration and any support as we work together to make America even greater.

God bless America and help us all make her better!

Chapter 2 How to Run for Public Office

Making the decision to run

There are lots of how to's and to do's when one finally decides to run for public office at any level. There are official and unofficial documents that can help in making the decision. They also aid in helping the prospective candidate know what to do. All the write-ups by well-meaning government entities are written in a way to sweeten up the candidate's idea of running for office so that they will choose to run.

These are not bad sites. They do not tell prospects for candidacy not to run for office because "your friends will think you are a jerk." But, they might as well say that. Just like my friends, your friends will question your motivation and they will question your ability to beat machine politics in any state.

For Pennsylvanians considering the plunge, there is a wonderful fact-filled write-up that appears to have been written by the state. It is hosted by Wyoming County, PA. You can get to it online through your web browser by typing in *wycopa running for public office*. The actual URL web address is complicated so use this search argument in a search engine and it will better help you access the document.

Much of what I present in this chapter is from this document plus I throw in my personal experience as I also do throughout the chapters in the book. I went through the whole process as a neophyte in 2010 when I ran for Congress, once again in 2012, as I ran as a write-in for the US Senate, and once in 2015 as I ran for Mayor of Wilkes-Barre, PA.

You might say that I have had my fill of such instructions and following them to the letter of the law. But, I am at it again running for the US Senate in 2018 as a write-in candidate. I will talk about write-in options later in the various essays throughout the book.
When I ran for Congress in 2010, I got 17% of the vote and five years later in my home town, I got just 5% of the vote when I ran for Mayor. I also spent more money in 2015. I have learned many lessons. My net gain from all this activity is that I now get to say that I ran for office.

I am glad that I did, and I am running again but as a write-in, I will no longer have to spend large sums of money to get on the ballot and conduct any campaign. I run for office hoping to help the City or District or State in which I live handle the pressures of today more effectively. I know that I would do better than the likes we wind up electing time and time again.

A side desire of mine has always been to get rid of the machine from controlling government at all levels to help bring the government back to the people. So far, I have been unsuccessful because the system is definitely rigged. Yet, I continue to have hope that somebody will emerge to take on the bad guys and bring the people a victory. Maybe one day it will be me. Maybe it will be you. So far, it looks like our best hope is to find more people in the country like Donald Trump.

It surely does not have to be me. I would love for everybody who once thought about running for office and hopefully is thinking about doing so again, to promise they will never vote for another two-term incumbent. That is a first step in making the process fair. The people have to get rid of the existing bad guys or as many like to say, "Throw the bums out!" It can become a fair system but not without help from the people at election time. It won't change until we throw out the people that made it like it is.

Government, my friends is bad because we have elected scoundrels to offices that are important for all the people. Additionally, a SWAMP of officials from after many years of service to government who, though employees, begin to operate on their own for political reasons. Good personnel systems and people are needed to get rid of them.

The fact But, the people we have elected in many if not most cases have become greedy and self-centered. They have distanced themselves from the needs of their constituents and the people they sear to serve.

One of the most important things that a prospective candidate for office must do is a self-evaluation. You must be sure that you are ready both for the possibility of success and the probability of many disappointments along the way.

Unfortunately, a prospective candidate for public office using traditional methods also needs to determine if he or she can afford the commitment of time, money and energy necessary to run for the intended office.

Though the official documents make it seem like it is 1, 2, 3, the fact is the incumbents have made the process unnecessarily difficult. Therefore many, once engaged think they cannot really run for office. Expect obstacles and you will not be disappointed.

Let's suppose for a minute that you are certified Mensa (The High IQ Society), but you have minimal resources and even less cash. You are going to have a tough time without donors.

To be successful using the traditional approach of getting on the ballot is very difficult without a pile of money. In my case, running for Congress, I had to buy a lot of yard signs and other material to help myself become known. It cost me about $5000.00 in 2010 and I took no donations to remain free of political encumbrances and entanglements. I wanted nobody to own me. In retrospect, I was too strict as family donating $50 or $100 each would not create an issue.

In addition to money, a prospective candidate must also make sure that he or she is qualified to hold the office being sought. There are no listed qualifications to make sure this is really true, however. My rule of thumb is that if you think you are qualified, you are.

Once you have assured all this, and you want to proceed, your next step is very important. You need to check in with your family and friends, especially your immediate family. You must make sure that they are OK with your running for whatever office. In my case it was Congress. I got reluctant acceptance from my immediate family, which told me that it was OK for me to proceed.

You then need a team of good people to help you. You cannot do it alone. The only thing you can do alone in life is fail. You will need people who can think with you and people who can do work for you. There is lots of work from placing signs, creating fliers, speeches, and essays, building a website, and going door to door to get petition signatures.

You also need one very, very good friend, or if you have some money to burn, a good campaigner who will work for you and be paid to organize your campaign. In my case, Marty Devaney, a very good friend of mine understood the system and he worked very effectively with me. He donated his time and effort to the cause. He was my campaign manager and a great man.

Marty and I put together a team of about forty people from my friend and family group. My brothers and sisters were not happy with the idea and so only a few helped me in the grassroots work. Thankfully, I had a great team of friends and in-laws who were pleased to host a few events and participate as needed as we organized our approach. You'll find that people bring in other people when the benefit to all is better government.

This gave me about three team captains and I could have used more to assure things like signs and nominating petitions were completed. A number for my high school friends asked to help so in the end we had a formidable group. One of the great measurements of our campaign success was that we got over 1500 signatures in three weeks and less than forty were stricken as invalid.

What should first-time candidates know?

I gave you the search argument for the document you should print and read (wycopa running for public office). Pay close attention to the instructions provided and check out all the forms necessary to gain ballot access. Make to-do-lists as you read the documents.

In addition, if you plan to spend more than $5000, or if you have more than $250 in expenses, as a first-time candidate, you need to become familiar with the Campaign Finance Reporting Law, which is posted on the Department of State's website atwww.dos.state.pa.us/campaignfinance.

You might want to ask a friend who is an accountant to help you in this regard, even if they charged you as the details on this huge report are tricky. Remember, all of these things are hoops in a gauntlet that you must traverse in order to be deemed qualified to get on the ballot to run for office in PA.

A prospective candidate should also understand the commitment of time and energy necessary to run a successful campaign for public office and no matter what you thought it would be, it will be even more because incumbents do not ever want to lose and they make the rules.

Try getting on the ballot but make sure you are ready to work harder than it ought to be.

What a candidate must file to access the ballot

Signature requirements vary depending on the office for which the nomination petition is being circulated. The rule of thumb on signatures is always get twice the number you need. For example, when I ran for Mayor, I needed 100 signatures. My little team brought in over 250. When I ran for Congress, I needed 1000 signatures. My expanded team brought in over 1500 signatures and we checked them thoroughly to make sure there were no gotchas. We lost only 40 in Harrisburg when they were examined by state officials.

You must inform the state what office you are running for and assure they send you a campaign packet with the needed forms before the three-week period for signature gathering for your nominating petitions. You can get your packet early, but you cannot solicit signatures before the declared first day.

Obviously one of the forms you need is the nomination petition. If the heading information is not filled in properly, an entire petition can be thrown out during the inspection process when you turn them in. In other words, make sure everything is done right or you can lose as many as 50 signatures in one clip.

Below are some forms you will need. They should all be in your packet. To be sure you have the right contacts in the state to get the packet, visit your county election bureau (voter services) and tell them you are running, and they will review what you need. In some cases, depending on the office which you are seeking, such as Mayor or Council, the County group will have all the forms you need.

For governor or senator or Congress, you will need to get them from the state. The county people will tell you how to get them. When you visit the county ask about getting the CD of voters' names & addresses, so you know who is Democrat and who is Republican. If your office spans counties, ask the county voter services head in each county for their CD. When I ran, there was no state-wide CD.

If you are a Democrat for example, running as a Democrat, you need to get signatures of only Democrats. Republicans get Republican signatures on their petitions. If you are running for a slot on both tickets, you need to get the minimum number for each party to be on their respective ballot ticket in the primary. The form you use for getting signatures is called a nomination petition. Forms are described below:

The Candidates Affidavit
Each candidate must file with his or her nomination petition or nomination paper an affidavit setting forth information about the

candidate, including the candidate's residence, election district and the name of the office the candidate is seeking.

The Statement of Financial Interests

The Statement of Financial Interests is a form that must be filed with the State Ethics Commission, which requires the filer to set forth information regarding the filer's sources of income. A copy of the completed Statement of Financial Interests must also accompany the nomination petition of a candidate for state, county or local public

The Nomination Petition

Each page of a nomination petition contains three basic components: 1) the Preamble; 2) the Signatures of Electors; and 3) the Affidavit of Circulator.

The Preamble:
The preamble is the portion of the nomination petition page where information about the candidate is inserted. The preamble includes the office for which the candidate seeks nomination, the name of the candidate, the candidate's occupation, the candidate's residence and the party affiliation of the signers.

Signatures of Electors:
Each person who signs a nomination petition must insert the following information about himself or herself: 1.-Signature; 2.-Printed name; 3.-Address of residence, including street and number, if any; and 4.-The date on which he or she signed the nomination petition

The Affidavit of Circulator:
Each nomination petition page must include the duly executed affidavit of the person who circulated the nomination petition (the circulator). The circulator of the nomination petition page must swear or affirm the following:

That the circulator is a qualified elector of the Commonwealth or of the district, as the case may be.

That the circulator is a duly registered and enrolled member of the political party designated in the nomination petition;

That the circulator's address of residence is as set forth in items 4 and 5 of the affidavit;

That the signers of the nomination petition page signed with the full knowledge of the contents of the nomination petition;

That the signers' residences are correctly stated on the nomination petition page;

That each signer signed on the date that the signer inserted next to his or her signature, name and address of residence; and

That, to the best of the circulator's knowledge and belief the signers are qualified electors, who are duly registered and enrolled in the political party designated in the petitions and are residents in the County set forth in item 1 of the affidavit.

Sorry I had to do that to you in such detail, but it is a game rigged for regular citizens to withdraw rather than proceed.

Please note that unless you are superman, you will need multiple circulators for your petitions. These are the people who ask other people for their signatures. Make sure the circulator information is done correctly above. You may have five circulators and each of them may have various nominating petitions. For example, a circulator may get 50 signatures and then need another petition form. A circulator may choose to keep one at his family residence and in the office and in the car, etc. Each has to be filled out properly. Your opponent would be pleased to find a flaw in your work.

Challenges to Nomination Petitions and Nomination Papers
The system is set up that if John W Public writes John Q Public on the petition for any candidate and it is later proven he is John x Public, his line does not count. If your write an abbreviation for Wilkes-Barre as WB or W-B, that signature or form does not count. Pay attention to the rules. I have a copy of the handout sheet I used for circulators at the end of this chapter.

Entrenched establishment politicians like Joe Sestak or Bob Casey, Jr. will challenge regular guys such as Carl Romanelli or like Joe

Vodvarka, hoping to scare them into not running. Typically, an individual such as Sestak can challenge the validity of a nomination petition by a good guy like Vodvarka within seven days of the filing deadline for nomination petitions or nomination papers.

Sestak has already challenged the petitions of Vodvarka because he cannot stand the thought of a guy running against him, and he apparently has the resources to squash Vodvarka rather than let him run.

The Candidate List

If you change your mind after you are on the ballot, there is a last day to withdraw or you will be on the ballot regardless. As a valid candidate, you will be asked to come to the state capitol for Congress as an example to draw lots for ballot position. If you do not want to go to Harrisburg for example, the Capitol Police will draw your ballot. I chose the latter method and luck of the Irish, I was listed # 1 on the ballot.

After the last day for candidates who have filed nomination petitions to withdraw and after the candidates have cast lots for position on the primary ballot, the Secretary of the Commonwealth must forward a list of statewide candidates of each party to the various county boards of elections. This is how your county knows you are on the ballot.

A candidate of a minor political party or political body will have his or her name placed on the November ballot upon acceptance of his or her nomination paper by the Department of State or the County Board of Elections, as the case may be, unless the nomination paper is judicially set aside as a result of a successful challenge to the candidate's nomination paper. If you fit in this group, please spend some time talking to some experts to make sure this is done properly. Most of what we have discussed so far is how to get on the Primary ballot.

CAMPAIGN FINANCE REPORTING

Who Must File Campaign Finance Reports/Statements?

Campaign finance reports/statements must be filed by candidates for public office setting forth information regarding contributions received and expenditures made for the purpose of influencing the outcome of an election. A candidate may also authorize a committee to accept contributions and make expenditures on the candidate's behalf. The committee must have a chairperson and a treasurer, who may not be the same person. Each candidate and each authorized political committee must file reports of receipts and expenditures, if the amount received or expended or liabilities incurred exceeds $250. Otherwise, the candidate or the treasurer of the authorized political committee may file the statement in lieu of the reports. Candidates are required to file a campaign finance report/statement that is separate from the report/statement

ELECTION DAY

Electioneering
No person, including a candidate, may electioneer or solicit votes when inside a polling place. All persons, except those persons authorized or be inside the polling place (election officers, clerks, machine inspectors, overseers, watchers, persons in the course of voting, persons lawfully giving assistance to voters, and peace and police officers), must remain at least ten (10) feet from the polling place during the progress of voting.

Watchers
Each candidate may appoint two watchers for each election district (polling place) in which the candidate's name appears on the ballot. However, only one watcher for each candidate may be present in the polling place at any one time.

Candidates interested in appointing watchers should contact the appropriate county board of elections for information about submitting the names of watchers and obtaining certificates for those watchers.

Qualifications of watchers:
Each watcher appointed to serve in an election district must be a registered voter of the county in which the election district is located.

In order to serve as a watcher, a person must receive from the appropriate county board of elections a Watcher's Certificate, which the watcher must present when requested to do so.

Rights of Watchers:

When a watcher is not serving in the election district for which the watcher was appointed, the watcher may serve in any other election district in the county in which the watcher is registered to vote.

Watchers may be present in the polling place from the time the election officers meet prior to the opening of the polls until the time that voting is complete, and the district register and voting check list is locked and sealed, provided that they remain outside the "enclosed space" (the area in which the voting compartments are located).

A watcher is permitted to keep a list of voters and is entitled to challenge the qualifications of a voter in the manner provided by Law. Watchers should take care to issue challenges in good faith. The Pennsylvania Election Code does not authorize wholesale or frivolous challenges, which are intended to intimidate voters

Chapter Appendix My personal rules for signatures

I developed and used this instruction sheet in my 2010 run for Congress. I have made it more appropriate for 2018. These are not state rules. They were my rules and I gave each circulator and anybody part of the team a copy to help avoid mistakes. When I created this "cheat cheat," I made it one sheet. Look on

www.briankellyforcongress.com web site, the main menu for a pdf of the form called Signature Rules.

Rules for Signatures -- Brian Kelly for Congress 2010 Page 1

1. Get a clipboard, & Black Pen. -- I should have enough here. Put your stuff in the clipboard

2. Get at least one sheet for each county (Luzerne, Lackawanna, Monroe, Columbia, Carbon) in which you may choose to get signatures -- If your streets are in Luzerne County but Mom and Dad's are in Lackawanna County, you need two sheets. Take as many sheets as you think you need (50 signatures max per sheet)

3. Look at the sheet. Note that Item 6 is the County. Luzerne is filled in on some sheets. If you go to counties outside of Luzerne, before getting any signatures fill in the County Name. Do not mix people from different counties on the same form.

4. Look at the sheet. Each sheet holds 50 signatures. You are to observe the person filling out the signature line. Use just one line each to sign and complete their line on the petition.

5. Look at the sheet. The top of the sheet page 1 is already filled out other than county in some cases. [I did this when I copied the forms for Luzerne County where most of my circulators were] The note to the Secretary of the Commonwealth is next. This describes what the signature / line is all about. It is not a vote. It is your agreement that a fellow citizen (me) in the 17th district may run for Congress.

6. Look at the sheet. Lines 1 to 29 and heading. Space for 29 signatures on Page 1.

7. Look at the sheet. In the signature space this is how the signature and information are to be printed / signed. Ditto marks are not permitted anywhere.

A. **SIGNATURE OF ELECTOR** -- Each signer of the nominating petition is an elector -- i.e. one who has a right to vote D (Democrat) in the primary and is in District 17. (If your case is Republican, make sure the signer is Republican – do not mix Ds and Rs on same sheet) Observe the signatory sign in that space. The signature itself must be in cursive form - not printed.

B. **PRINTED NAME of ELECTOR** -- Caution the signatory that the name in the signature and the name printed are the same name - initials or no initials etc. Observe the signatory print their name the same as on their official records -- such as driver's license. Use middle initial if on license.

C. **PLACE OF RESIDENCE - HOUSE #-** Observe just house # printed in this space.

D. **PLACE OF RESIDENCE - Street or Rd**. Caution the signatory to place the street or rd with the designator st. rd. or ave. followed by apartment # (apt 1) if there is such a #. Observe the signatory type this information. Street, road, or avenue may be abbreviated but not the street name.

E. **PLACE OF RESIDENCE - City, Boro, or Twp**. Caution the signatory to use no abbreviations for the municipality. For example, WB, W.B., W-B, W-Barre are all invalid and will cause the signature to be thrown out.

F. **Date of SIGNING**. Observe the signatory print the date while cautioning that it must be correct and within the period of February 16 to March 9, 2010 (check the dates).

For example, 02/16/2010 is valid and 02/16/2009 is not. Any date such as 02/15/2010 or before this date is not valid. Any date such as 03/10/2010 or after this date is not valid.

Any mistakes on date will cause the signature to be thrown out.

Circulators should make sure that the dates on the form are oldest to newest sequence. March 8 should not be before March 1 on the form. Examples below use a random date.

AA. Note on the signature line --- >> If the signatory makes a number of mistakes and it does not look good. It will not be accepted. Draw a straight line through the whole line and ask them to start over on the next line. Do not waste lines.

BB. Lines 30 to 50 are valid spaces for signatures -- thus each sheet can hold a maximum of 50 signatures (29 on front and 21 on back). Get as many forms as you need!

CC. Each Saturday beginning February 20 (pick date), please call D. Greemez with the # of signatures that you obtained that week.

The sooner we get all the forms to Harrisburg the better. 655-5555. Or email <greemez@comcast.net>

DD. On February 27 or March 6, depending on how we are doing, all forms need to be brought to BK's house (candidate) and we will have them notarized. We will have a notary onsite to do this. He or she will do them all at once and charge BK, not the circulator. Circulators must be present to sign in front of Notary

EE. On March 2 or March 9 BK will take the notarized forms to Harrisburg. If you cannot come to get the forms notarized, please have them notarized in your area and BK will reimburse you the expense. BK will come to your house to pick up the notarized form, hopefully before March 2.

FF. Look at the form on the back in the affidavit of circulator. You are the circulator. Do not fill this out the left side at all and do not fill in the right side until all the signatures are on the sheet and the Notary Public is standing in front of you.

GG. Make sure Brian gets as many forms as possible filled with signatures and that they are notarized either at the meeting on Feb 27 or March 6 or by you and your own Notary.

HH. Some have asked for data sheets. Get your data sheets now! Tell Brian what streets / towns you want if your sheets are not ready. Verify that the person signing actually signs their name as it is listed in the data sheet or their Driver's License (should be the same)

II. Can you get anybody's signature? Yes, they know if they have previously signed for Brian so don't worry about it. Get the signature - Democrat -- District 17. Make sure County is correct on the form -- If you get signatures from 5 counties, you need 5 forms.

Review: Many signatures are thrown out because of small mistakes.

Let's Look at the areas of mistakes that might be made for the meeting

1. Make sure that every detail of everybody's signature is perfect

2. Do not use WB or ditto marks.

3. Make sure you use the Luzerne County form only for Luzerne County Signatories

4. If the signatory makes a mistake, draw a line through it and let them write it again.

5. It helps to check the data sheets vs. the signatures line for errors.

Why would a signature be contested? Here's why:

Signature Line Challenges -- the incumbent or other challenger wants to get all signatures thrown out claiming inaccuracies

1. Date on line not between Feb 16 & March 9
2. Signer is not a registered voter
3. Signer resides in wrong district (16 or 18)
4. Signature or data not completely legible -- ask them to do-over.
5. Multiple counties on same form – entire form gets thrown out.
6. Address is wrong / incomplete / missing address
7. Incomplete / missing dates / dates out of order
8. Ditto marks
9. Nickname or initials in place of full name
10. No cursive signature
11. Wrong / fraudulent signature*

Write notes on your notes such as these:

 *** We will have a meeting at my house on Feb. 27 or March 6, depending on how the signatures are coming in. I will bring a Notary public to notarize the signature petitions for the carriers. BK will pay for it. Do not get them notarized before then.

Don't forget to ask your relatives, close friends and those who you see all the time. We are looking for D, D17

Send Greemez an email so he can communicate with you
<greemez@comcast.net>

Chapter 3 Ballot Access: The Game is Rigged!

Try running for office!

Contact: Brian Kelly for US Senate
Email bkcampaign@yahoo.com
Date: April 13, 2018

****** PRESS RELEASE ******

Like you, Senatorial Candidate Brian Kelly is disgusted with the current leaders in our government. He is asking for voters to forget about what big government can do for them. The results are in and the verdict is "0." Kelly is asking voters to write him in -- in 2018 for the US Senate.

Brian hopes to help release our wonderful country from the grips of the socialists and communists.

In this essay, Brian Kelly demonstrates the difficulty for non-politicians (regular Joe's), such as him, to gain ballot access in a system designed of, for, and by corrupt incumbent politicians.

His essay title is:

BALLOT ACCESS: THE GAME IS RIGGED!

Please enjoy this essay by Mr. Brian Kelly.

Try running for Office in a state such as Pennsylvania, in which the political Incumbents and the establishment have the game rigged. Pennsylvania's corrupt state politicians have slanted the ballot-access table in favor of incumbents and against non-political regular citizens of the Commonwealth.

There are major trials and tribulations facing regular people who attempt to present themselves as candidates on any ballot for any office in the United States of America. The ballot access issue in Pennsylvania is one of the worst in the nation. It should not surprise anybody that the incumbent politicians make the laws that make it difficult for anybody to unseat them. There are many surprisingly restrictive ballot access laws in this country. The average citizen voter has no knowledge or concept of the extent of the problem until one day, he or she decides to put their hat in the ring and they run for office, hoping to give something back.

If you are so inclined, do you feel that you might actually be able to run unimpeded for an important office in Pennsylvania? Would you just go ahead and do it or would you be concerned that the weight of the political machine might be too heavily focused against your candidacy? If you gave it a shot, do you think you would be permitted to run unfettered against a well-established political class whose livelihood and whose continued excessive wealth depends on being elected continually until they die?

I thought I would run for office simply because I am an American and this is America. I have done so but let me tell you the road is unpaved. I ran for Congress and for Mayor. I was on the ballot for Congress in 2010 and on the ballot for Mayor of Wilkes-Barre in 2015. There is a lot of work in running for office and unless you become a politician, or the people stop bootlicking politicians by voting for them, a new candidate can expect nothing but misery and failure.

Do you wonder why so few people run for office? Surely you have neighbors who you think would be much better at leading our country, state, county, or city than the same old crew whose names make the ballot every election. I know first-hand why more good people choose to stay away from becoming elected officials. It is because the politicians control the playing field. If you think the game is rigged, you are right! The game is rigged.

There is a big reason why potential candidates for office do not simply emerge into the sunlight when they are so inclined to be the next Mayor, Governor, Senator, or Representative. It is the same reason that even Donald Trump and Bernie Sanders have learned in trying to become president. The game is rigged, at all levels.

The reason is that there are lots of impediments and major roadblocks that need to be carefully navigated. Those currently holding offices of and for the people, think they own the people. Consider that there are no documented cases of an elected official, who in their first term or any term ever calls all citizens of the community together for a meeting to find some other good candidates to run.

It seems logical that we all would have been invited at some time to say, a church hall, so that a great leader could describe to us the process of becoming the next such and such from so and so. If we all wanted the best people to serve, would we not be encouraging our neighbors to come out and be welcomed to consider putting his or her hat in the ring to serve the people?

Why are we deprived of having regular, ordinary citizens such as you and me, rather than machine groomed politicians be the candidates for the offices available in almost all elections? The answer is that over time, the political class through gerrymandering and restrictive ballot access laws, and special rules known only unto them, have made it difficult for anybody other than a crooked politician to get elected.

Politicians play the game and they eventually become experts. It is not by accident that the winners are almost always endorsed by the big Party machines, and let me tell you all, the machines are really big and are really powerful and tough to overcome. Regular Joe's and

Josephine's are excluded in the process intentionally, but the methods are not entirely obvious. The fact that it costs a lot of money to compete is just one of the first obstacles.

For the money and the major effort, a newcomer has less than a slim chance to gain the nomination or win a general election. Once you put your hat in the ring, there is a lot of unexpected and unnecessary work and expense. It is not an accident that any candidate running for the first time feels that all of the politicians and the minions in government have their hands locked into his or her wallet.

It was not always that way and the founders did not intend it to be that way. Unfortunately, elected politicians have always had the power to make things easy for their next election regardless of its impact on democracy, the will of the people, and the good of the people. The founding fathers expected that the people would throw the bums out, but the bums have made it very difficult,

Their path to a reelection and a slot at the establishment perks table is much easier than your path to be newly elected. They use something that I would call a special "incumbent grease." The incumbent grease makes them quite slippery and it helps them to be impervious to the rot they create, through which those not as well connected must traverse.

It was not until the 1880's for example that paper ballots began to be printed by the government. Before then it was private entities who produced the ballots and even before then voice votes were used. In the 1880's official secret ballots came into being by government decree and that is when the ballot access issues for John Q Public began. It is funny how the government broke a system that had worked well for 100 years at that time. Government breaks a lot more than it fixes.

The elitists believed that only elitists should be able to run for public office and they set out to make sure that it was a task that most ordinary citizens would choose not to take up. Today as we see in Congress and the Senate, and even the Presidency, the sense of entitlement to the office held is so strong that the "elite" politicians believe that they know more than the people they serve.

They also know that it is so difficult for a newcomer to replace them that they no longer believe they have a requirement to do the people's will to be re-elected. Of course, that was before the recent populist movement that has Donald Trump and Ted Cruz and Bernie Sanders, ostensibly outsiders to the presidential process, doing so well today. To not be an incumbent in 2018 is now a major advantage for the people. But, will the establishment still have the power and the gall to direct the results? We'll see!

The TEA Party movement of 2009 from its first brew was unfairly defamed by the corrupt progressive media. Yet, it is the TEA Party, a term not mentioned much today that built the foundation for today's populist movement. This movement has brought us candidates who do not owe their allegiance to big donors or the Party machines.

Wikipedia, which sometimes, but infrequently, gets it wrong, got this fact 100% right. It cites that historian Peter Argersinger pointed out that the 1880's reform "that conferred power on officials to regulate who may be on the ballot carried with it the danger that this power would be abused by officialdom and that legislatures controlled by the established political parties (specifically, the Republican and Democratic Parties), would enact restrictive ballot access laws to influence election outcomes, for partisan purposes, in order to ensure re-election of their own party's candidates." Peter Argersinger was 100% correct and my own story as a candidate confirms that.

As a candidate several times who paid a big price to be on the ballot, I can assure all Americans that the ballot access system provided by the states is not designed to let the most competent person through the maze. Thus, the people most often send the same scoundrels back to office rather than helping new blood present its case. First of all, there are no ready forums to present one's a case.

One would presume with no knowledge that the United States would have the fairest ballot access rules in the world of countries that practice a form of democracy. But, this is not true. The United States has been criticized by the Organization for Security and Cooperation in Europe (OSCE) for its harsh ballot access laws in the past. From my own experience, the US has not really lightened up on the rules that prevent ordinary citizens to get on the ballot. The corrupt press never reports on it as it is part of the problem, not the solution.

This is one place in which it appears the Brits have us beat. In their political science model of a healthy two-party system, every candidate for Parliament faces the same ballot-access hurdle-- a simple filing fee. Not only is it free but candidates from all parties are granted two free mailings to all the voters. That's not the end of the fairness. Every candidate also gets some free TV and radio time. It's almost as if the Brits want real people not just politicians to be able to achieve an office in Parliament.

We have the same access here if you have the big bucks and lots of spare time. In Britain, they have legal equality between all the parties and it seems to work. Our system seems to be corrupt. As Donald Trump says quite well and quite often: "The system is rigged." Trump is right!

You saw what happened in Colorado, Trump said. It's a fix. We thought we were having an election and a number of months ago, they decide to do it by you know what, right? They said well do it by delegate. Aw, isn't that nice? And the delegates were all there waiting. And, one of them tweeted out today and said today, by mistake, and then they withdrew it, something to the effect of See, never Trump.

Mr. Trump spoke at a rally with over 10,000 supporters who packed the Times Union Center, a sports and concert venue in downtown Albany: I'm hundreds of delegates ahead but the system, folks, is rigged. It's a rigged, disgusting, dirty system.

As a person who has run twice in this dirty system, I more than agree. It is rigged to benefit long term dirty corrupt politicians who in this election, are known simply as "The Establishment."

Even at the local level, when I ran for Mayor in 2015 and was on the ballot, I requested in early 2015 that Mayor Leighton open City Hall for a meet the candidates night twice a month for the few months of the election season. Each mayoral candidate would speak for an hour and each Council candidate would also get time to speak.

The Mayor said the City could not sponsor such events as it was against the law. I have two sons who are lawyers, and this simply is not true. Regardless, the Mayor acted like he owned City Hall, not like he was merely renting it with the people's permission until the end of his term. I beg to differ that a Mayor or public official cannot choose to help the electoral process.

But, we all know it is very difficult fighting City Hall. The newspapers are AWOL. Radio stations permit call-ins for brief periods but the local TV stations including Public TV offer nothing for aspiring candidates. The message is to get your wallet out and pay to permit the people to learn to know you. The Fourth estate is dead in Wilkes-Barre PA and for the most part across the country.

In 2010, when I ran for Congress, the incumbent, who seemingly was responsible for funding allocations for Public TV, decided that there would be no public forum or debates on Public TV for the Congressional House Race! Is it not convenient to be the well-known incumbent and have the power to limit your opponent's opportunities to take your job?

The noted scholar John Henry Wigmore, professor of law at Northwestern Univ. from 1901 to 1929, who ultimately was dean of the law faculty had some big-time opinions on fair elections. In his earlier life (1880s) Wigmore had been a leader for election law reform, especially the secret voting method and ballot access laws. His suggestion in my opinion makes sense. He recommended that as few as ten signatures would be an appropriate requirement for nomination to gain access to the official ballot for a legislative office.

For Congress in PA, a candidate needs 1000 signatures plus 1000 more signatures to cover signature challenges. For Senator, one needs 2000 signatures plus 2000 more. For Mayor, one needs 100 signatures plus 100 more to cover challenges. I dare you to try to get a signature from anybody for anything. See how easy it is. Candidates get three weeks to get all signatures while still going to work every day. Each signature petition sheet of 50 maximum and 1 minimum must be notarized. That is another $5.00 to $10.00 per signature.

So, does that make Pennsylvania law 100 times better than the suggestion of this sage legal scholar who thinks ten signatures are sufficient? Let me repeat myself on the requirement. As noted, in PA, one hoping to become a candidate on the ballot for Congress on the Republican or Democrat side must attain 1000 signatures plus 1000 more for challenges in less than three weeks. I submit that this is regardless of how many snow storms there may have been. All of this hard work, 100 times more than Wigmore's suggestion is necessary to be a candidate for US Representative for either party. Incumbents illegally use their staff to get the signatures or the Party pas as much as $5.00 to $10.00 per signature to have professionals canvas for them. Regular citizens have no such staffs.

At about six to ten signatures per hour, one certainly cannot expect to hold a job and live a normal life if trying to get the signatures by oneself. The clear objective of such as system is to limit the access to the ballot so that normal people say, "no way," and politician after politician has his or her way with the people's treasury.

When the signatures are submitted, it is also clear that the objective is to eliminate signatures, not to verify the real citizens who signed the petitions. They may be valid citizens, thereby making their attestation valid but if they make a mistake in their own name or the city or the date or their apartment #, their attestation of a candidate is thrown in the garbage. In the current US Senate primary in Pennsylvania, Joseph Vodvarka's signatures are being challenged by the opportunistic Joe Sestak.

When I first wrote this essay, Mr. Sestak hoped to deny Pennsylvanians a candidate who is of the people and not of the political class. He hoped to chop hundreds of signatures from Vodvarka's submitted petitions. He wanted them marked invalid so that Mr. Vodvarka would lose his right to be on the ballot. That's how bad it is. Since then, I learned that on April 1, the Courts favored Sestak. What a sham. The system is rigged.

Sestak almost immediately took Vodvarka to court, so it will cost Vodvarka money to defend his petitions with over 2000 signatures. Sestak, a well-tuned in politician says more than 60 percent of the Vodvarka voter signatures is not known for being a handwriting expert. Yet, he claimed the signatures were flawed and should not be counted. I say if they can find ten good signatures, Vodvarka should be in! Try getting 4000 signatures in three weeks.

Most courts are smarter than the politics often employed by jurists in making decisions. The PA Court ruled against Vodvarka.

U.S. Senate candidates have a tougher time to get signatures than House candidates. Instead of 1000, they need to collect 2,000 signatures to qualify to be on the ballot. Those petition signers must be registered to vote in the county where they reside and be of the same political party as the candidate. Joe Vodvarka had submitted 2,744 signatures, which ought to be enough, except in a rigged system, to have him on the ballot.

Prior to the Commonwealth Court hearing argument on Sestak's challenge, attorneys for Vodvarka and Sestak reached an agreement and stipulated to the court that 558 signatures on Vodvarka's petitions were invalid. As long as he was on the ballot, why would Vodvarka care that he only had 200 or so to spare. That left Vodvarka with 2,186 signatures. But the Commonwealth Court chopped off another 400 signatures so Vodvarka could not run on the ballot with 1800 signatures. What kind of guy does that make Sestak? What kind of lousy system would authorize such a perpetration of justice?

Political pundits have often said that the poll tax is the worst tax possible as it denies people the right to vote. It is my humble opinion that the method of using exorbitant numbers of signatures and arbitrary signature cancellations is worse than a poll tax as it denies the citizens the very candidates that would make an election with just politicians running, into a real election. A politician's objective, such as Joe Sestak, is to eliminate candidates not to verify that they are capable of serving.

Speaking of taxes, to help get 1000 signatures, one can ask for the county database or state database. I called the state and was routed back and forth and then each time; the phone was conveniently disconnected. For my part, I got the pleasure of dialing again but since time is important, I chose not to work with the state. The state database cost $20.00 or so I had been told.

District 11 [Before the recent changes to District 17] in Pennsylvania consisted of all or part of five different counties -- Carbon, Columbia, Monroe, Lackawanna, and Luzerne. To get the databases for these counties, they must be obtained from the counties one by one, for a sum of $50.00 per CD or $250.00. To capture one signature on a petition in each of the five counties--a total of just 5 signatures--would cost approximately $10,00 in Notary Public fees per sheet or $50.00 to have all five signatures notarized.

Why is this a requirement when the State does not accept the notarized affidavit---the word of the Notary, anyway? Vodvarka's were all notarized but the court did not accept the Notary's attestations. The answer is because it is effective harassment for anybody who dares challenge the powers that be. But, you already know that.

Of course, each House petition holds 50 signatures, so it would take 20 perfect petitions to reach 1000 signatures at a cost of $200.00. Since, at least 1500 signatures are recommended as many will be eliminated rather than verified, this cost is at best $300.00. With signature circulators working on behalf of every candidate, many of the sheets have no more than ten signatures. Of all had just ten signatures, this would be 100 sheets and the cost would be $1000.00 for the notarization of the signatures.

What purpose does this serve?

Additionally, there is a filing fee of $150.00 to be able to submit the petitions and be duly registered as a candidate to be placed on the ballot. They don't take Visa or Master Card. They do not take personal checks. So, I had to go to the bank to get a $150.00 cashier's check made out perfectly to the State of PA or they would not accept it. More harassment. Then, though there were five Voters services offices in District 11, ostensibly because this is a National election, the full petition, a notarized affidavit (another $10.00) and the cashier's check had to be taken to Harrisburg (two hours each way plus mileage cost -- say another $50.00) to a specific room to be processed.

In the directions from Harrisburg, to add insult to injury, I found it comforting that there was a caution after noting that the signature period was from February 16 to March 9. The caution said, "Do not wait until the last minute." In other words, the office is closing at 5:00 P.M. on March 9 so you better be in, processed, and out by 5:00 P.M. When I arrived on a Tuesday, I thought I was OK. Only about forty signatures were discounted. Despite all the obstacles I made it onto the ballot. .

Many citizens do not know how difficult it is for a non-politico to run for any office in Pennsylvania or they would insist that the rules be more reasonable. We have our corrupt state lawmakers to blame for that and they must fix this even before, in our contempt for them, we replace them all. I will do my best, I can assure you to enable ballot access for all so that we the people are not cursed to have only politicians to choose from in our elections.

Speaking of citizens and the requirement for 1000 signatures. It is my understanding that the incumbent merely instructs his staff to get signatures and it is not that big of a deal. If the staff is only minimally involved the incumbent can attend a number of political events during the three-week period with hundreds of willing signatures available at each event. The lone wolf, the average Joe, our own John Q. Public, does not have it quite so easy.

In my case, I called a number of establishments to see if I could bring my petition inside and quietly ask people to sign to help grant me ballot access. I learned something in this process. Some establishments are quite gracious and assist in this civic duty of enabling ballot access for citizens of NEPA, who are not part of the machine.

Of course, they would also permit those of the machine and that is fair. Some establishments are not so gracious and they either put me off or took it up the flagpole only to have the owner decree that they did not engage in such politics. For me in these cases, I concluded that they had an alignment with the machine, which I did not have. Knocking on doors is the toughest way to get signatures.

I am running for the US Senate in 2018

Until I die, I may continue to run for some political office. What I will not do is spend money or raise money. I will have a web site, write articles, send editorials to newspapers, and I will speak when invited.

When elected to the US Senate this year, I will serve one term and If I am in good health in six years, I may go for one more. That ought to be more than enough.

I spent close to $5000 of my own money to run for Congress in 2010. When I ran for Mayor in 2015, I thought it would be easier. I spent about $6000 but family and friends donated about $3000 so altogether, I am out at least $8,000 and probably more because of PA ballot access laws. I won't do this again this way for sure. I wish I had the cash back for a few family vacations. Yet, here I am running for office. How am I going to pull that off? Quick-answer -- Write me in!

If voters tuned into write-in ballot laws, and there was a listing service so that anybody could announce that they were running as a write-in candidate, we can again have a democratic republic as the founders intended. It costs nothing to run as a write-in. All you have to do is make sure that the potential voters know about you. So, with the listing service, instead of having to get 1500 signatures, anybody can run for Congress. Because it would be so easy and be no charge, citizens would have a huge selection of candidates. We should talk more about this... don't you think?

In the meantime, I bought a web site to handle write-in ballots. Well, it really does not handle write-in ballots as you still have to vote at your polling place. However, it is a place in which any write-in candidate can list his or her name so that any citizen can access the site to find out who they are. That way, ladies and gentlemen, we are not stuck with politicians as public officials.

The name of this web site is www.writeinballots.com. I have yet to fire it up but some day!

God bless America!

Vote for the Underdog... Just write in Brian Kelly this time. It's that easy! Next time send out a memo like this, and we'll all be voting for you and it will not cost you a dime I think!

With 165-books, Brian W. Kelly is the most-published and thus the leading conservative author in America. He is an outspoken and eloquent expert on solutions to help America and Americans Though a Democrat, he is a JFK Democrat. One of his pet peeves is the chicanery and deceit of RINOS and DINOS on all Americans.

About Brian Kelly:

Brian Kelly is a former IBM Senior Systems Engineer and Retired Professor of Business and Information Technology (BIT) at Marywood University in Scranton, PA. He was a candidate for US Congress from PA District 11 in 2010. Kelly was also a candidate running for Mayor in his home town of Wilkes-Barre PA in 2015. Brian still manages his own IT business (www.kellyconsulting.com), and he has recently completed his 165th book, available at amazon.com/author/brianwkelly.

Brian is currently running for office as a write-in candidate as a Democrat for the US Senate to Pennsylvania. You can check out his campaign web site at www.kellyforussenate.com). The good news according to Kelly is that when running as a write-in, there are virtually no campaign expenses.

Thank you for being part of the quiet populist revolution to save America.

Chapter 4 Elect Brian Kelly as your US Senator for Pennsylvania

Do you have what you need to assure Brian Kelly is your right guy for the US Senate in 2018?

Whenever any company or organization evaluates somebody for a position with the company, in addition to a cover letter, and the compulsory employment application, most professionals are asked to provide a resume. In Academia, that resume is called a curriculum vitae, and seemingly, the bigger and thicker it is, the better it is for the candidate.

I know from teaching in colleges and universities for thirty years that academics enjoy puffing themselves up--sometimes literally. Go to a college graduation and look at the plumage as the PhD's are all gussied up in their finest academic garb, checking out each other's pedigree.

A resume is often as simple as a one-page biography (bio), the typical form one uses to gain a consulting contract. A business resume is rarely more than several pages. "Curriculum Vitae" is from the Latin and to be short .it means "life's work." When you see my curriculum vitae, you will be able to tell that it includes everything including the kitchen sink. Technically it is to be a brief account of a person's education, qualifications, and previous experience, which is most often sent with a job application. As noted, in academia, however, the document is often more than just a few pages.

About ten years ago, I made the transition from a business resume to a curriculum vitae when I became a member of the faculty of Marywood University as an Instructor. Eventually, I was promoted to Assistant Professor and a few years later, I departed the University for various reasons. This permitted me to devote more time to writing and to my other professional consulting endeavors.

A curriculum vitae therefore, is often a large document which includes a summary of educational and academic backgrounds as well as teaching and research experience, publications, presentations, awards, honors, affiliations and other details. If you are curious, you may read my most current vita. If I were to choose to apply again, I would update it at

http://www.briankellyforcongress.com/files/bkcvnov172014.pdf Feel free to save the pdf of my resume so you do not have to absorb it all in one sitting. Enjoy!

Since I am running for office as a write-in candidate for the US Senate in 2018, I will explain how to vote for me in subsequent pages. Before I do that let me tell you some more about myself so you know that you are making an informed decision.

About Brian Kelly

Brian Kelly is married to the former Patricia Piotroski and the couple resides in Northeastern Pennsylvania as they have all their married life of forty-one years. They are the proud parents of three wonderful adult children, Brian, Michael, and Katie. Ben, the family canine, and Buddy, the family feline, reside with Pat and Brian, but are loved by all.

Brian Kelly was born and "raised" in Wilkes-Barre PA. He attended St. Boniface Grade School and Meyers High School. Brian was both a pitcher and a catcher on the Meyers High Baseball team and he was active in many school clubs as well as the student council.

Brian competed for an academic scholarship to King's College and was awarded a four year academic scholarship grant, a National Defense Student Loan, and a work-study job. The job in the federal work-study program helped him make up a $50.00 per year shortfall. Tuition was $475.00 per semester. Scholarship was $250 and loan was $200. Brian is most grateful to King's College for the Academic scholarship and to the Federal Government for the loan and work-study assistance. it was the difference between a successful business life and a blue collar job.

Brian graduated cum laude from King's with a degree in Data Processing, the pre-cursor degree to Business Information Technology. While at King's, Kelly was a member of two honor societies, the King's Aquinas Society, and the Delta Epsilon Sigma National Honor Society. Brian played varsity Baseball for the Monarchs as a catcher / pinch hitter, and then as a starting pitcher in his Junior and Senior years.

After King's, he joined the IBM Corporation as a Computer Science Systems Assistant where he spent 23 years before retiring, under a special program, as a Senior Systems Engineer. During his IBM career, Kelly received his M.B.A. summa cum laude in Accounting and Finance from Wilkes University. After his time at IBM, Brian accepted a position with College Misericordia as its Chief Technology Director / Internal IT Consultant. At the same time, he initiated his own IT Consulting Practice, Kelly Consulting.

After building the College Misericordia campus network, its connection to the Internet, its email and its Web servers, Kelly left College Misericordia and moved on to spend full time in his own IT business consulting practice. In 2004, Kelly joined the faculty of Marywood University and, in addition to maintaining his consulting practice, Brian served Marywood as an Assistant Professor of Business Information Technology and as its IBM i system technology assistant to the Business Information Technology Faculty.

Contact campaign@briankellyforcongress.com

An Entreaty to vote for Brian Kelly from Brian Kelly

Fellow Citizens of Northeastern Pennsylvania, I would like to present myself as a Candidate to be your US Senator for the State of Pennsylvania. As you know, this seat is currently held by Bob Casey Jr. but not for long. I am running as a write-in candidate, a Democrat against Mr. Casey in the General Election on November 6, 2018.

I am proud to say that--but for a few years as an independent living in Utica, NY, I would be a lifetime Democrat and a lifetime resident of Northeastern PA. Right after I earned my Bachelor of Science from King's College at the age of 21, I competed in a tough job marketplace, and I had the good fortune of being hired to work as a Systems Engineer at IBM in Utica, New York. For two years, I lived in Utica as a registered Independent.

My dad, a lifetime Democrat, was very conservative and good man. He was a staunch believer in the importance of labor unions to help the working man in America. He worked as heating specialist at R. A. Davis in Wilkes-Barre and then as laborer at Stegmaier Brewery on "Brewery Hill" in Wilkes-Barre for thirty-one years until the Stegmaier label was purchased by the Lion Incorporated. At that time, the Lion proudly brewed Gibbons Beer.

[G-I-B-B-O-N-S, pure refreshing Gibbons. If it's Gibbons, it's good—so the next time you should say gimme gimme gimme gimme Gibbons!]

That is the essence of the 1960's Gibbons commercial.

Stegmaier of course brewed a number of different beers, including Stegmaier Beer, Ale, Porter, and Bach. When I was in my twenties, the "Brewery" brought back Liebotschaner, a finely crafted and aged old-time Stegmaier formulation. The company made its beer from fresh grains and hops and malt and it aged all of its products in huge vats on the left side of Market St. as one headed up Brewery Hill.

[So! If you want a beer that's mellow, a beer that is really grand, say hey, make mine Stegmaier, the gold medal beer of the land. And, so at home, or club, or tap room; always order the beer that they cheer. Served just right; mellow, cool, and light, Stegmaier Gold Medal Beer.]

This is the essence of the 1960's Stegmaier commercial.

My dad was pretty good at what he did, and he took his work seriously. For a number of years before its demise, Stegmaier had one of the fastest canning machines in Pennsylvania. My dad operated this behemoth single-handedly. For its day, it was an awesome machine. It put out 600 cans per minute. That's even fast according to today's standards. My dad was quite a guy.

My father and I regularly had discussions about beliefs and ideologies and which candidate truly was best for official jobs, at the local, state, and federal levels. More often than not, he and I were on the same page. My dad's philosophy was that you should always vote for the best candidate for the job, not simply the political party. These discussions eventually prompted me to cancel my registration as an independent, and become a Democrat. In Pennsylvania, Independents have no voice in the primary elections.

Lots of discontent is not only brewing; it's boiling-over.

There is a storm of discontent content brewing across the United States. You can feel it wherever you go. Regular Americans are beginning to pay attention to what our Congressional representatives have been doing against our will in Washington, D.C. Politics and government, and their collective effect on what's happening in America have become regular dinner table topics.

I know few people today who thought President Obama was a good president. In fact, most of my friends see him as the worst president ever. I think they are right! Sometimes particular Democrats do not have it right. It is OK to be upset. It is OK to show some disgust for what these knaves such as Bob Casey Jr. have done to us. It's OK to be disgusted, Me too! That's why I am running for the US Senate.

The leaders of the Democratic Party have betrayed the common man, such as you and me, but none of us writing or reading this paragraph are dead and so we can change the Democratic Party to no longer be the party that separates Americans under the guise of diversity. Instead for the sake of American Unity, we can all join together under the huge umbrella of the US Constitution and reject those leaders who have led us down a path to perdition.

What's not OK is to sit around and let these same elitist establishment types come back again in 2017 to inflict more harm on the American people. Vote them out. You have the power! We have the power!

I decided to run for the US Senate as a write-in candidate because somebody has to represent US. I am a write-in because it means that I do not have to bootlick the rich and powerful for donations. We need change more now than when we thought we needed change and brought in Obama. God gave us Donald Trump as a model for how things should be done.

What we do not need is the kind of change that exalts one man and attempts to silence a nation. I ask you to vote "for the people" on November 6 of this year. Vote out the proponents of big, intrusive, freedom-taking government and all the politicians will disappear overnight.

It seems the kind of change we have been getting from our former anti-American President and the corrupt Congress was good only for the government and the high-paid bureaucrats. It is not the right formula for freedom-loving Americans. While you and I are asking to have government less involved in our daily lives, Congress and our former president were throwing one freedom-stealing regulation after another on us on their way to making this a socialist nation. This Congress does not represent the people.

We can fix that. All we have to do is vote them out. The people think that they are powerless, yet we have all the power. I am running for the US Senate and I am a Democrat. Please do not vote for anybody who has hurt Donald Trump's presidency in the general election.

Don't count on other states to get this job done without our participation. It all starts at home. For US, that is Pennsylvania. Our time has come. Good-by to all the incumbents who are contributing to the downfall of America. Good-by to Bob Casey, an embarrassment to Northeastern PA. Hold your collective noses and then vote him out!

I would hope that by learning about who I am and where I am from and what I stand for, you will conclude that we have unity of purpose. I am one of the regular people in life. I believe that it is my time to serve and if you will permit me, I would be honored to be your Senator for all the regular people in Pennsylvania.

Things that are worth repeating are worth repeating

Here is some stuff from a press release by the campaign that is very readable and as most of Brian Kelly's writings, it calls the people to action. Brian believes that we the people have no choice than to be more than mere passers-by in a country being drugged into submission by people who hate America.

*** PRESS RELEASE ***
BRIAN KELLY ANNOUNCES HIS CANDIDACY FOR the US SENATE FROM PENNSYLVAMIA.

Kelly Says It Is Time to Return the Government to The People!

Brian Kelly, a former IBM Senior Systems Engineer and Assistant Professor of Business and Information Technology (BIT) at Marywood University in Scranton, announced his write-in candidacy for the US Senate .

Kelly has promised that he will run as an independent write-in candidate in the general election in the event he does not win the Democratic Party nomination. Brian asks all white Democrats to vote for him in the general election as he will serve all voters well.

Brian Kelly has worked in the private sector all his life. He hates what is happening to the US and to Pennsylvania and his solutions are designed to make it better.

Are lawyers in elected office ever good for the people?

Having two sons who are practicing lawyers, please know that I what I am about to write has to do with lawyers thinking they own the people. My sons are fine young men who represent their clients well against insurmountable odds.

Can't we do better than sending a lawyer to Congress? You may know that only about 5 percent of Americans have ever thought about running for elected office, according to a 2002 survey. Yet another survey shows that 58 percent of lawyers have considered the idea. Why should the rest of us want to be governed by lawyers? Lawyers are in fact nothing more than politicians in waiting. We can do better than sending a politician or a lawyer back to Congress.

They ask the question: What is the difference between a dead skunk in the middle of the road and a dead lawyer in the middle of the road? Who would ever know the answer but a lawyer… A lawyer of right mind would say: "There must be tire skid marks in front of the skunk."

Some others via email ask questions like "How many lawyer jokes are there? And of course, the answer is "only two." The follow-on is that the rest of the jokes are true stories."

Even law school students, and I should know because I provided snacks to both of my children, both of whom are great lawyers, while they were attending law school. They paid their own way and had some student loans. My boys know that many lawyers forget their oaths.

From what they learned at home, my children intrinsically know that lawyers are a negative breed of their own. As a group, they are dishonest and mean, deceitful and spiteful, arrogant and oblivious.

Even other lawyers think other lawyers are not trustworthy. Not every single lawyer, but most of them. The exceptions don't change the rule. Nobody would consider putting a bouquet of roses on a pile of manure to reduce the stench? It doesn't work. Lawyers are at a minimum not respected in society unless they have provided some specific benefit to some specific person. Most humans expect that lawyers will expel an unpleasant scent.

Brian Kelly expresses his reason for running for public office in these simple terms: "to return our government back to the people." Kelly notes that government spending is out of control and that only a change in leadership can turn government away from more unpopular tax-payer funded bailouts, crippling taxes and government-takeovers. Casey, a successful lawyer of course is for more spending and for more taxing of those who earn a living in Pennsylvania.

Brian sees the solution as "We must create jobs, not destroy them. The policies of Bob Casey and Barack Obama were killing US businesses before Donald Trump was elected. Like many, I fear the building of a huge, never ending bureaucracy wherever you look." Brian believes that Bob Casey must go so a Trump-Friendly legislature can be in place to help America.

Kelly finds government as the only "industry" prospering. He deeply fears the seemingly predestined government takeover of healthcare, the disrupting of the doctor patient relationships, and the bankrupt notion of repressive energy tax legislation and the destruction of the industry that produces America's most abundant energy source-coal. He is concerned that all of this excessive government, which the incumbent supports, will make it tough for Americans to live like Americans. "You can be assured that I will work to stop these flawed changes brought about by poor leadership." Kelly said.

Kelly said that in order to restore the economy, "a brand-new Congress must be committed to getting government to stop micro-managing the economy."

Government takeovers, national debt, a huge deficit, and the major job killing regulations of the Obama / Casey administration are being rejected summarily by all Americans.

Pennsylvanians will be hurt even more than others by the shutdown of coal and an "energy tax" since many PA communities still have a viable coal industry. Casey is not for Pennsylvanians and his votes could kill the energy industry in PA though taxes or restrictive regulations.

Besides being unfriendly to Pennsylvania business and industry, the only creators of lasting jobs, Bob Casey is vulnerable in 2018 because his positions mirror those of the unpopular Chuck Schumer, Nancy Pelosi, and Maxine Watters. Why would our Senator, against constituent write-ins, support Obamacare and other socialist, budget busting legislation?

Kelly boasts that he has the backing of no political machine and he is taking no political contributions. "It sure should save a lot of time, not having to run fund-raisers." Kelly said. He is proud to say that his total war chest from contributions is $0.00, and he is nowhere close to having to pay the "Obama / Casey Rich Tax."

Kelly feels his message will be brought forth now that he has made it known that he is a serious contender for the nomination and for election in November 2018. By writing in the name Brian Kelly, the people will recognize that a regular old "John Doe," not a political operative has made himself available to the people.

Kelly once had a lot of affinity for the "Tea Party People," and those like you and I, who are not part of a named group but who nonetheless have been justifiably enraged at the unresponsiveness of our government. From Kelly's perspectives, the left made the tea party seem like a bunch of life perverts and nobody complained loud enough to know they that it was not the tea, it was the name and it was the people, regular people who the left hoped to discredit but could not because they were simply you and me. .

Kelly said: "At this stage of my life, I see things that can be so much better if Americans had better representation. I feel in many ways like George Bailey from the Building and Loan in "It's a Wonderful Life," seeing the face of the corrupt Mr. Potter in too many hallways of government.

I'd like to take the spirit of WW II Brigadier General Jimmy Stewart (real life) as George Bailey and keep all the Potters out of government for an awful long time--even if it means that I have to put in a few years myself."

Kelly is not interested in a career in politics and when elected will stay for just one or at most a few terms. Kelly says: "A regular person holding an office becomes a politician when trying to be reelected."

When the constituents of Pennsylvania get in the "voting booth," no matter how many dollars Bob Casey has spent to advance his candidacy, the only thing voters must remember is two words forming one name, Brian Kelly. It is just ten letters and a space. When they write that name in BRIAN KELLY on the ballot, things will begin to change almost immediately.

"The voters will ask themselves, 'is he a politician?' and the answer of course is 'no.' As voters across the US are trying to free themselves from machine politics, with votes to the highest bidders, Brian Kelly is betting that in Northeastern PA, being 'of the people' will matter more than anything on November 6, 2019. " Kelly said.

As an author, Brian Kelly wishes he were not so old that he has been able to write 165 books, many of which are in the high-tech field. He is tickled, however, that he has written twenty-one books since 2010 hoping to convince his fellow Democrats that we must not permit the power brokers in the Democratic Party to ever win again. We can still be good Democrats if we force the power brokers to be more human.

In 2007, Brian Kelly began research for his first book about government. In 2008, he released these first efforts with a book titled, Taxation Without Representation, sold on the Internet at such places as Amazon.com and Barnes & Noble. He has updated the Taxation book and wrote many new patriotic books since then.

These are the product of major research as well as his clear opinions as to how the country has gotten off course. Two of his newest books include Wilkes-Barre PA Return to Glory! and The Constitution 4 Dummmies, and Millennials are people too !!! . Those who think the thoughts of the people do not matter, will not read any of these books

Kelly is an ardent defender of the Constitution and in many of his books, he adds appendices with the full text of the US Constitution and other founding documents.

By visiting this website at www.kellyforussenate.com or by reading his books, available at amazon.com/author/brianwkelly, it is easy to know that Brian Kelly stands where you stand on the issues of the day. He sounds like one of US because he is one of US.

Brian Kelly asks all Democrats and Republicans in Pennsylvania to write-in Brian Kelly in the General Election on November 6. Two words, both are needed for a valid write-in. "I promise that you will have change --- this time it will be change that you can live with." And, won't that be a grand day. ---------

Best wishes for a better America from Brian Kelly.

Sometimes it helps to see things again in summary form:

Brian Kelly's Summary Background:

- E. L. Meyers High, W-B, PA, with honors
- B. S. from King's College cum laude
- M. B. A. from Wilkes University magna cum laude
- 23 years with IBM Corporation as Senior Systems Engineer
- 15 Year Ongoing Consultancy--Business and IT Consultant
- 5 years Misericordia University, Chief Tech Officer
- 7 years with Marywood University -- Assistant Professor, Business Information technology
- Author—165 books, Hundreds of magazine articles

Brian Kelly believes in the effort to restore reverence for God and respect for the unalienable rights to life and liberty in America.

Brian Kelly believes and understands the notion of self-government of, by, and for the people – as well as our moral, physical, and economic sovereignty. Kelly has written four books in this regard:

Taxation Without Representation; *Obama's Seven Deadly Sins* - ; and Healthcare Accountability. Included in each of the first three books is a full copy of the Constitution of the United States, something that we all should keep in our hands in these trying times. Kelly penned another book titled: <u>Jobs! Jobs! Jobs! in 2010.</u>

Altogether he has written 165 books. Most were penned between 2010 to 2018. All are available from amazon.com/author/brianwkelly

Brian Kelly is easy to understand. He is in synch with the Donald Trump agenda. He is an advocate of a complete overhaul of our taxing system and the abolishment of the 16th Amendment, thereby eliminating the tax code and the IRS. The Fair Tax has many advantages over the current income tax system. The Fair tax seems to have the most advantages of all other options, but even the Flat tax is far better than our current income tax system

-
- Brian Kelly is an advocate of strong border security
- Brian Kelly is ready to declare our nation's reliance on God as fundamental.
- Brian Kelly will work to protect our unalienable rights to life, liberty, and private property.
- Brian Kelly will help restore and protect our constitutional republican form of government.
- Brian Kelly will work to protect the institution of marriage and the traditional family.
- Brian Kelly will work to protect our national sovereignty, military strength, and border security.

The rest of this book describes Brian Kelly's candidacy so that as had been announced in the past by those against Mr. Kelly, nobody can say that Brian Kelly is not the best candidate for America.

Chapter 5 Why is Brian Kelly Running for the US Senate

Question: Why are you running for the US Senate?
Answer: That is a very good question?

As a husband and father, my family was very important in this decision. In 2008, I considered running and my family and I discussed it at length and I decided not to run. In 2010, I put a team together, and I saved some money and my family gave me encouragement, though they still had some trepidation about the potential impact on our family unit. We'd like to remain reasonably private and regular people. At the same time, there were other factors.

This year, eight years after having the #1 position on the ballot for the Democratic Primary, I am running for the US Senate as a write-in candidate, because of a number of reasons. I am running as a write-in because I simply cannot afford to try to outspend the fat campaign war-chest amassed for Bob Casey. So, I am running a campaign on the cheap but with your help, I will prove that money does not trump the will of the people.

My family agrees that things are even worse for Americans this time around. I would be happy to defer my candidacy to a like-minded person if one shows up. Short of that there are a lot of things that are wrong, with our country, and I would love the opportunity to get my hands dirty to help fix them. I am at the right time of my life and I see no reason why I should stand by and watch as my family's liberties, both economic and civil, are being wiped out by our own government.

Reagan had a sense of humor

You may remember Ronald Reagan's great sense of humor. Reagan, for example is credited with a number of sayings. Without me offering any commentary, you can learn a lot about why I am running for the US Senate from the fact that I really do love the following Reagan quotes.

"The nine most terrifying words in the English language are: 'I'm from the government and I'm here to help.'"

"Approximately 80 percent of our air pollution stems from hydrocarbons released by vegetation, so let's not go overboard in setting and enforcing tough emission standards from man-made sources."

"I've noticed that everyone who is for abortion has already been born."

"I am not worried about the deficit. It is big enough to take care of itself."

[Brian Kelly adds that Ronald Reagan never met Barack Obama]

"Politics is supposed to be the second-oldest profession. I have come to realize that it bears a very close resemblance to the first."

Does that help you know where I stand on those issues? There is a whole menu on this site. It is called "Platform Points." It discusses just about any point in my platform and offers where I stand on it.

In life, we are often told that we must be for something, not just against things. I am for a lot of things but one of my best ways of describing why I am running for the US Senate is to speak in the negative. "I do not want the government controlling my life." Yes, there is a corollary to that precept: "I do not want the government controlling your life."

I can recall some great people in my life making comments that now make so much sense. For example, Dennis Grimes Senior from Fulton Street in Wilkes-Barre, who, when told that Congress did not get much done this term, would always say: "good!" Then, of course with the twinkle in his Irish eyes, he would add a little priceless gem to make the sentence end well, and I would smile. How profound he was.

Each time Congress meets we lose more freedom. There are too many people who think that you should do this, and you should do that. It is bad news when they get into office. They want to make sure you do it and they have the power to make laws to make it mandatory. I want to let you alone to lead your own life, and I hope if you are in similar circumstance, that you will let me alone to lead my life.

I believe that freedom is our most important gift. Our forefathers shed their blood for our freedom and liberty. Freedom has no real limits but being a good person does add restrictions to freedom.

For example, I believe that in many and possibly most cases, a particular individual's freedom ends where another person's freedom begins. So, there will always be disputes between people and so it is OK to have some rules that help arbitrate man's behavior to his fellow man. My favorite rule book was created by the Founders. It is called the Constitution. Barack Obama and the 111th through 115th Congresses think they know better than the rules in this book and that is one major source of the angst in this country.

The fewer impositions of government on the people, the better. Government should get out of lives. We can handle salt, and sugar, and heat and cold. Government should worry about roads, bridges, traffic, and defense and a few other limited items.

I see no reason, for example to have a government law that outlaws beer, or two-ply toilet tissue, or red hair, or tattoos. I see no reason for laws that command that I must do something such as attend church services on Sundays -- or not attend or turn off my air conditioner in the summer (car or home) because somebody else wants me to save energy. I would not want to be commanded to use Dr. X as my family physician instead of Dr. Y. I surely would not want to have a visit scheduled with Dr. Kevorkian.

I would not want to have to use gasohol when gasoline or an alternative energy source suits my tastes. I would not want to have to buy health insurance, a pair of mittens, blue socks, a notepad, or cough medicine if I am not so inclined. I want liberty. I want freedom to make my own choices in life. On everything but abortion, I am pro-choice. On this issue I am pro Mom and pro Baby!

For me, it really is all about freedom, which is the positive of "no government control." I do not want government monitoring or controlling of my life from womb to tomb or any other area in between. I have written sixty-some additional books between my first run for Congress and now, many of which include a full copy of the Constitution of the United States.

The Constitution was created in order to form a "more perfect union," since it corrected a number of flaws in the Articles of Confederation. It is not perfect, but it is lots better than Nancy Pelosi and Chuck Schumer and Barack Obama, a trio who have no problem making up freedom-destroying rules on the fly, as they go along.

My campaign is a very new campaign and for many it will not seem like much of a campaign. That's OK, the founding fathers would love it. If the truth be known, there is no real "campaign," just a bunch of friends who help me with great advice and my very active keyboard where I pen letters to the editor, press releases and essays for my web site. Thank you for reading this one. I hope to be able to select some "free" events in which to participate, but they are not offered frequently as incumbent politicians know that the more you know about me, the less you will like them.

The vast percentage of the people I know believe that we must fight back against a monstrous, out of control government. Those who know me believe that I would make a difference in Washington, and though they have cautioned that nobody gets elected without putting together at least a little machine, they enjoy the fact that we are doing this without any machine and with no contributions.

In 2010 my little team and I went out over three weeks and brought in 1516 signatures though I needed only 1000. Only! Try and get them. I will never do that again as I had to shut down my life and the lives of too many friends. We were out getting signatures but since all of us have some type of gainful employment, we could not have an exhaustive campaign and did not and will not try to knock on doors. It is tough enough just penning these articles.

I ran once for Congress and once for Mayor of Wilkes-Barre and so I will make some mistakes. My Web site is still out there though it has some misspellings and I may say things incorrectly as the site is eight years old.

www.briankellyforcongress.com

It is true that most voters (rightly) mistrust their Congressman and Senators. My plan is to be one of a new breed that puts the ordinary person first. My plan is to listen to the people of Pennsylvania and work to help make the founding principles, the very best principles for our country, as the best solutions to make all of our lives better. That's the way it is supposed to be.

Though I am a Democrat, I am very people oriented and very pro-American. Americans first! I have no use for the radical hard left, whose influence is undermining our democracy. As a constitutional conservative democrat, I will work to get us back on track while always listening to the people to know when more track or a few switches are needed.

Thank you for "listening." Don't forget to vote on November 26, 2018

Chapter 6 It's Tough Being Unknown!

"THE BIGGEST MISTAKE YOU COULD EVER MAKE IS BEING TOO AFRAID TO MAKE ONE."

~UNKNOWN

-EmilysQuotes.Com-

Everybody knows somebody sometime

It is not such a good thing when "everybody knows somebody sometime" and you are not on the list. When you are the new guy, sometimes the press forgets.

Many of my friends have asked me how I hope to get known in the sixty-seven counties that make up Pennsylvania. Let me tell you, it is tough without major political financing. But, I will persevere with press releases, letters to the media, and I would be pleased to make a speech whenever asked. To get the attention of the Press, a candidate must first "press" his nose against the glass of the media outlets (Newspaper, Radio, and TV) to get their attention. I am doing that with this book and a number of press releases and letters.

Unfortunately for unknown and not-well financed candidates, in my experience in having run unsuccessfully three times, the priority of the management of media outlets is to maintain their viability by bringing in ad revenue and not giving up space or time to citizen candidates. I know that it will not be smooth sailing, but nothing ventured, nothing gained.

Fortunately, I can set up and manage web sites and I can use Facebook. Therefore, I can reach web surfers without any cost. This time, I will not have a Donate Button to accept contributions but that is OK as I won't need an accountant when it is over to figure out the financial statements. Because it is a state-wide election yard signs in the local community will not be effective, so I will save on that.

In their article, Journalism in the Digital Age, five Stanford (cs.stanford.edu) authors-- Danny Crichton, Ben Christel, Aaditya Shidham, Alex Valderrama, Jeremy Karmel, take the time to explain the absolute importance of a Fourth Estate (the media) as the most important pillar of our Democratic Republic:
Here is what they say:

"Journalism has long been regarded as an important force in government, so vital to the functioning of a democracy that it has been portrayed as an integral component of democracy itself. In 1841, Thomas Carlyle wrote, "Burke said there were Three Estates in Parliament; but, in the Reporters' Gallery yonder, there sat a Fourth Estate more important far than they all" (On Heroes and Hero Worship).

Four years earlier, Carlyle had used the phrase in his French Revolution: "A Fourth Estate, of Able Editors, springs up, increases and multiplies; irrepressible, incalculable." Carlyle saw the press as instrumental to the birth and growth of democracy, spreading facts and opinions and sparking revolution against tyranny.

"The fact of the matter is that democracy requires informed citizens. No governing body can be expected to operate well without knowledge of the issues on which it is to rule, and rule by the people entails that the people should be informed. In a representative democracy, the role of the press is twofold: it both informs citizens and sets up a feedback loop between the government and voters.

The press makes the actions of the government known to the public, and voters who disapprove of current trends in policy can take corrective action in the next election. Without the press, the feedback loop is broken, and the government is no longer accountable to the people. The press is therefore of the utmost importance in a representative democracy. Today, the press is more concerned with making fake news than with reporting real news, so it will be a tough challenge indeed.

"Another, related, function of the press is to expose people to opinions contrary to their own. This function is perhaps the most valuable in the Internet age; while people can in theory get information about the actions of their government from online sources, it is all too easy to find opinions online that match one's own. Informed decision-making on the part of voters requires an awareness of multiple points of view, which is not likely to be obtained if voters bear the sole responsibility of seeking out information on relevant issues.

The news media provides a forum for debates to take place, as well as moderating and curating the arguments presented by all sides. It is, of course, idealistic to suppose that media give equal, or even proportional, representation to all opinions, but the fact that many media outlets present themselves as nonpartisan sources of information makes them a better forum for debate than online sources such as blogs, which are typically maintained by one individual or a small group of people with similar opinions..."

It would be nice if the mainstream media took the time to provide forums in their media to inform the public of the candidacies of all citizens running in all elections. Even if it were not every day, and the media used its power to permit short speeches to be carried on their on-line sites. The media's job in our Republic is to inform the public and let me just say they can do a far better job. When you consider that in the three times that I have run for office, the media was mostly MIA, I can say I know from experience.

I have not even been interviewed or permitted to participate in any event on Public Television, even though we the people pay for it. I was interviewed when I ran for Mayor on Election Day but the channel

WBRE TV in my home town chose not to run the video. Let me repeat, the media does a disservice to the community by not informing the public of its choices.

I have never been endorsed by any media outlet as I have never been well known by their advertising departments.

Reporters and Newspaper Executives are not easy to move to your side. They do not feel obligated to assure that the public knows what each candidate has to offer.

The Press's problem in this general election season is that "Nobody expects that a guy 'who nobody knows,' will run for office." And so, I know that as a candidate, I will be very close to being summarily ignored.

I do not think that anybody in the Press tries to purposely hurt me or any other candidate, but they have their favorites. From my experience in the past, even after writing letters to the editor and sending multiple press releases trying to assure the media that I am a viable candidate, I found myself excluded from much of the news coverage. Whether it was intentional or not, no media outlet tried to make up for the loss of publicity my campaigns suffered.

I would hope that regardless of how well known a candidate may be in this upcoming election, the papers and the other news media of NEPA should permit candidates to do things that help the people become informed about where they stand on the major issues of the day. In the past, I have had few vehicles provided for me that would help the people know who I am.

Thus, anybody other than an incumbent or one well-endowed by blessings (cash) can expect to be relegated to the back seat in an election.

The papers. TV, and Radio etc. should permit candidates to submit a short essay, perhaps several times during the campaign. In some media, a short essay per week might be appropriate. In others, a mere mention every now and then would be very informative for the people.

The local government should also provide areas in which candidates can give speeches…but in my area, they do not.

The charter of the press is to provide news to the people, and news about who may be chosen to represent the people is worthy news indeed.

For me, the bottom line is that it is not easy for democracy to continue when the people have a tough time getting on the ballot and then they must fight against mythical forces to convince even their neighbors that they are serious in the endeavor. My political friends say that is the nature of the beast. I say, the beast is the problem.

An attentive press, concerned about the people, is very necessary to help a person not endowed by the machine to get their message out.

I do have a Web site, www.kellyforussenate.com. I thank you very much for visiting. I know that people do not just appear on this site. Most have to learn about it from some other media. Then, they can come to this site to learn about me and to learn why many believe that I am the best person right now for the job of representing Pennsylvanians in the US Senate.

I think they are right and I am working as hard as I can with the constraints that I have to help you know that I think like you do. Now that you are reading this paragraph, please write down the ten letters BRIAN KELLY on a sheet of paper and take it in the voting booth with you on November 6, 2018. Thank you. There will be a spot in which you can type in your candidate if not listed on the ballot. Simply type B-R-I-A-N K-E-L-L-Y. Please do not type the dashes though it might be OK.

Thank you for reading and / or visiting my site:

Chapter 7 Brian Kelly for US Senate Platform

Platform -- Influenced by Alan Keyes

In addition to the special platform points displayed in the announcement speech in Chapter 1, and the entire agenda of President Trump, please examine the following platform points to know more about your candidate.

As Brian was evaluating the items to include in the platform, he used the existing work of Alan Keyes, one of his favorite Americans. This assisted him in quantifying the issues of the American people. The following platform, however, is not that of Alan Keyes. It is Brian Kelly's platform, and as you know, Brian Kelly is hoping to gain your favor as the candidate running in Pennsylvania against Bob Casey for the US Senate from Pennsylvania.

Please read the items well as they are categorized in alphabetic order. The items within the categories are arranged in no significant sequence.

If you have questions or concerns about any of these, feel free to start a forum thread or send Brian an email at bk@kellyfoussenate.com. Thank you for your time and patience.

A. Abortion

1. A child has a God-given right to life from fertilization to natural death.
2. All unborn children are persons, not masses of flesh.
3. Abortion is "prohibited" in Declaration of Independence- prohibit abortion.
4. Embryonic stem cell research experiments with human life.
5. Human embryos in such research "gravely immoral" and unnecessary.
5. Need a Constitutional amendment defining life from conception.
6. Abortion is unjust and immoral.
7. Mothers have no right to take a womb baby's life.
8. Only exception is to preserve life of mother.
9. Brian Kelly is pro mom and pro-baby. No mom feels good after killing a womb baby.
etc.

B. Budget & Economy

1. Deficits must be eliminated.
2. Out-of-control spending must stop.
3. Budget must be balanced just like a household.
4. Balanced budget amendment to the Constitution is a great idea.
5. Need amendment to the Constitution to limit borrowing and spending.
6. No company is too big to fail.
7. If your business can't make it, expect no government help.
8. Government can have no stake in private enterprise (GM etc.).
9. No more bailouts period.
10. Eliminate "pork"
11. Cut Spending -- address the Debt

C. Civil Rights

1. Redefine separation of church & state according to Constitution.
2. Protect religion from the state, but not vice versa.
3. Right to acknowledge God is the foundation of all our rights.
4. Public display of the Ten Commandments is a state's right.
5. Official language of US is English.
6. Marriage is between a man and a woman.
7. Civil unions OK without the notion of or the word, "marriage."

C1. Affirmative Action

8. We cannot cure a past injustice with another injustice.
9. Preferential affirmative action patronizes blacks, women, other "minorities.'
10. Affirmative action is discrimination in reverse.

D. Corporations

1. Corporations should not have citizenship.
2. Corporations should not be permitted to become too big to fail.
3. Corporate mergers do not serve the public well-being.
4. Corporations should have plans to use American workers in America
5. Corporations should pay the social cost of "offshoring" jobs.
6. Corporations want cheap immigrant labor to replace Americans.
7. Corporate executives employing illegal employees should go to jail.
8. Incentives should be given corporations to not engage in labor arbitrage.
9. Workers' pensions need to be separate & protected in bankruptcy
10. Create two tier corporate income tax e.g. 10% domestic, 35% foreign
11. Tax penalty e.g. 20% for offshoring jobs
12. $5.00 per hour tax for each hour of illegal alien work.
13. Reduce foreign visas such as H1-B by 90% to save American jobs.

E. Crime

1. Death penalty is sometimes essential
2. Oppose "hate crimes" legislation -- redundant they are already crimes.
3. Harsh penalties for gang-related crimes in the same vein as RICO.

F. Education

1. Sex education is a private responsibility.
2. This is a Christian Nation.. Prayers to Christ or any god should not be barred.
3. Schools forfeit funds if they expose kids to gay propaganda / pornography.
4. Sex education if it exists at all, should be abstinence-based.
5. Relationship of college tuition rises & taxpayer subsidies is a big problem.
6. Funding for any agency promoting a political entity should be cut--Dept of Education was using taxpayers' dollars to promote the President
7. Teachers keep politics out of classroom -- no political indoctrination
8. Federal government may not use dollar incentives to affect state behavior. All states share equally according to population
9. Common Core -- Out! No Fed influence in education

G. School Choice

1. Parents & local citizens know better than educated masters.
2. Empower parents to choose schools that reflect their values.
3. Break up the government monopoly on public education.
4. Eliminate Department of Education -- use parental / local boards.
5. Pro-voucher; keep fed gov't out of K-12 education.
6. Money should follow parents' education choices.
7. Outlaw politically correct brainwashing.
8. Empower parents against the monopoly of public schools.
9. Let communities decide school rules-- such as all-male / female academies.
19. Make & Female restrooms

H. School Prayer

1. Who allowed the judges to drive God out of our schools?
2. Prohibiting school prayer creates a godless, anything goes society.
3. Christian schooling should receive tax credits. Religion taught off hours
4. Advocate prayer wherever you want in schools
5. God in schools may keep Columbine-like shooters out.
6. Constitution does not forbid prayer in schools.
7. Need prayer in schools and by educators.

I. Energy & Oil & Environment

1. Cap and Trade or similar legislation if enacted, needs to be repealed.
2. Need to seriously develop proper alternative fuels but do not force technology while fossil fuels including coal still work quite well. .
3. Drill here, Drill now in the meantime. Assure off-shore safety
4. Build clean and safe nuclear plants in the meantime.
5. Energy impact of hybrid fuels needs to be evaluated.
6. Ethanol burns more energy than it saves, and it raises food prices?
7. Explore & exploit ANWR, while respecting ecology.
8. Drill Offshore in all states that permit it.
9. "Global Warming is a hoax" so bad name changed to "Climate Change"
10. A Prophet should never make a profit" Al Gore - an approaching green billionaire
11. Against Copenhagen & Kyoto Treaty
12. CAFE standards kill people in crashes - abolish them.

J. Foreign Policy

1. Speak softly but carry a really big stick
2. Use common sense to make trade agreements that benefit U.S.
3. Evaluate the idea of not so free trade
4. Eliminate Trans Pacific (TPP)
5. Gain International concurrence diplomatically but act for the US
6. Recognize the UN as an anti-US agency.

K. Government Reform

1. Amendment for Initiation, Referendum, Recall at Fed level.
2. Give people a voice to overcome legislators' personal opinions.
3. Strictly limit government to the enumerated powers.
4. Focus on moral sovereignty, tax reform, & sealing the border.
5. No union or corporate or foreign donors to campaigns.
6. Disallow lawsuits that stop public officials invoking God.
7. Churches may identify candidates who favor its principles.
8. Congress should have last word, not supreme court
9. People through Initiation and Referendum get the last word.
10. Obeying the dictate of federal judges means no Constitution.
11. Less Government Control
12. Unlimited campaign contributions, but only by people, & well publicized.
13. Panel to examine constitutionality of executive orders
14. Congress can pick unconstitutional EOs without court appearances and eliminate them w/o Pres. concurrence

L. Gun Control

1. Fiercely defend the Second Amendment
2. Fundamental DUTY of free citizens to keep & bear arms.
3. Gun control mentality means crooks have all the guns.
4. Second Amendment not about hunting, but about national duty.
5. No federal role in gun safety-leave it to states & parents.

M. Health Care

1. Repeal all aspects of Obamacare including the "Porkulus" bureaucracy
2. Euthanasia violates unalienable right to life.
3. Patient in charge; no government-controlled health care.
4. No mandated health insurance and universal coverage.

5. Enhanced EMTALA and Enhanced Medicaid
6. Healthcare Accountability / Healthcare Loans
7. Eliminate pre-existing conditions, policy limits for insurance policies.
8. Protect disabled and vulnerable people like Terri Schiavo.
9. Encourage insurance reward for avoiding tobacco, alcohol, obesity.
10. People should take care of their own health.
11. Sensibly cap malpractice awards --- tort reform.
12. Health insurance purchases across state lines to reduce costs
13. Doctor / patient relationship key factor in any change
14. No Medicare cutbacks in treatment or access
15. Market determines health payments, not bureaucrats
16 Govt. becomes advocate for not v people.

N. Homeland Security

1. Peace through strength.
2. Strong & prepared military.
3. Eliminate political correctness from homeland security and the military
4. Assure Homeland Security Director takes mission seriously.
5. Assure Homeland Security Director believes we are at war.
6. Assure Homeland Security Director is competent.
7. Close up the border.
8. Penalize businesses who hire illegals before Americans - $5 tax per hour.
9. Stand unalterably opposed to all who commit terrorist acts.
10. Killing innocents by terror is same evil as by abortion.
11. Protect military chaplains' right to pray in preferred faith.
12. Allow Christian symbols in national war memorials.
       Country was founded as Christian!
13. No student visas to citizens of terrorist states.
14. Coordinate terror watch list with no-fly list
15. Doctrine of terror is killing innocent people.
16. Develop oil independence plan.
17. Drill Here. Drill Now!
18. Don't use Patriot Act to take away freedoms.
19. Send a clear message to the entire terror network.
20. Take preemptive action only if a probable threat exists.
21. Rapidly develop, deploy and/or enhance anti-missile defense systems.
22. Allies share cost of financing terror war efforts.
23. Supports missile strikes against terrorists abroad. (Aug 1998)
24. Establish an effective National Border Guard
25. Seal the borders of the United States

O. Immigration

1. Vigilant maintenance of our sovereign territory and borders.
2. Enforce existing laws against illegal immigration.
3. Sovereignty is betrayed when our borders are not defended.
4. Immigration, yes; colonization, no: oppose guest workers.
5. Control border first, or no other laws matter.
6. Blacks are hurt first by cheap immigrant labor.
7. Excessive multiculturalism weakens American culture.
8. Rescind Bush's order allowing Mexican trucks on US roads.
9. Oppose amnesty
10. Oppose guest workers until unemployment under 5%.
11. Extending privileges to non-citizens invites lawbreaking.
12. Expand orderly legal immigration as appropriate; curtail illegal immigration.
13. No U.S. citizenship for "anchor babies" of non-citizens
14. No immigrants from countries who are controlled of terrorists.
15. Pass something like a Resident Visa Plan and Pay to Go for existing illegals.

P. Jobs

1. Provide tax cuts to small businesses to help them provide real jobs
2. Encourage job creation as means to provide health insurance.
3. Work with corporations to undo damage of offshoring
4. Work with corporations to encourage jobs brought back to US
5. Penalize corporations that are bad citizens re: jobs. gov't contracts, etc.
6. No "sexual orientation" in Employment Non-Discrimination Act.
7. Government does not create jobs, only businesses do.
8. Family farms are nursery of moral character.
9. Create two tier corporate income tax -- 10% domestic, 35% foreign
10. Tax penalty to 20% for offshoring jobs
11. $5.00 per hour tax for each hour of illegal alien work.
12. Reduce foreign visas such as H1-B by 90% to save American jobs.

Q. Social Security & Medicare

1. Keep promises to those who paid so long.
2. Repeal the theft of $700 Billion for Obamacare from Medicare
3. Start Paying Back the SS & Medicare Fund -- generously
4. Tell the truth about COLA and CPI

5. Examine public land and offshore for energy as Social Security and Medicare funding source.

6. Oil companies pay the taxpayers for taking public oil.

R. Tax Reform

1. Repeal the Sixteenth Amendment.
2. Implement Fair Tax
3. Turn off spigot that funds politician's ambitions
4. Income tax has failed. Special people know the loopholes
5. Tax code filled with favors for special interests.
6. Replace income tax with a (1) national sales tax (FAIR Tax)
7. Abolish the income tax and IRS and spend money responsibly
8. National sales tax (Fair Tax) does give control back to people.
9. Augment taxing with tariffs & duties.
10. Income tax gives govt. too much control
11. Excise taxes allow citizens to control tax rate themselves.
12. "Soak the rich" schemes have un-American socialist objectives.

S. Technology

1. No Fairness Doctrine: no equal time if morally objectionable
2. Apply broadcast indecency rules to cable networks
3. Publicly fund NASA
4. Explore space aggressively -- Russia or China in Space is a threat.

T. War & Peace

1. Iraq / Afghanistan -- not best wars -- fight to win or get out
2. Use more technology and less troops.
3. Withdrawing before your enemy stops is called "defeat".
4. Need more countries to share the load
5. Do not go to war frivolously
6. Call Terrorism terrorism and fight it aggressively
7. Do not let Muslim immigrants into US until vetting procedures can be accomplished
8. Defeat ISIS big time by strength and cunning
9. Build areas within Syria & Mideast for returning immigrants to be safe.

U. Welfare & Poverty

1. Constitution does not require separation of church and state.
2. Charity to / from people, not from the government
3. Shift welfare from government to the faith sector.
4. Disintegration of the family causes social ills.
5. Encourage work instead of punishment if one parent goes to work
6. No welfare reward for having a baby.
7. Create a Welfare Accountability System for pay-backs

Bob Casey Jr. does not think like Brian Kelly.

Our country has already been sufficiently weakened. We must clean out all (not just some) of the corrupt anti-American politicians in Washington, DC. Senator Casey must be removed from office through the natural election process. Keep the faith. Good Americans can defeat this tyranny in our midst.

Chapter 8 Brian Kelly is a JFK Democrat

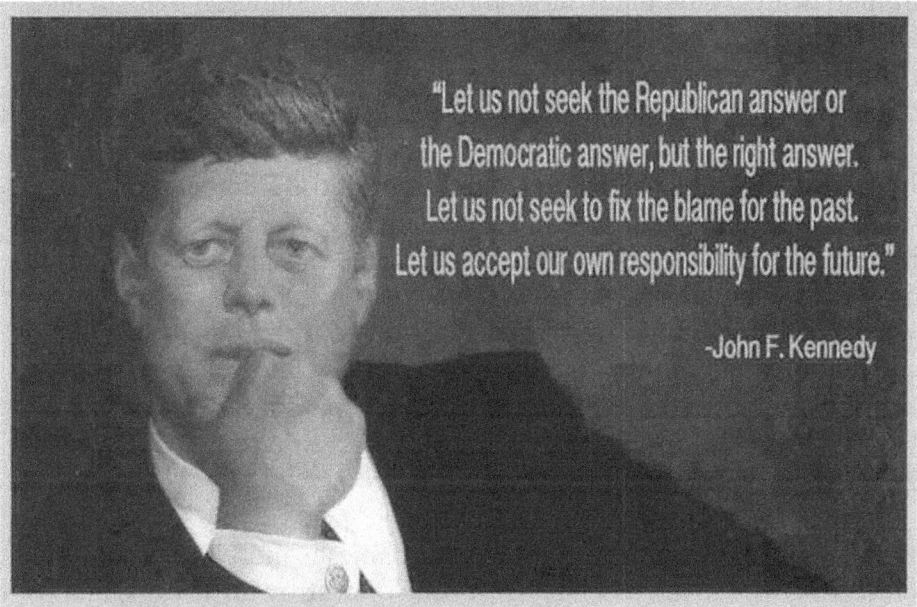

"Let us not seek the Republican answer or the Democratic answer, but the right answer. Let us not seek to fix the blame for the past. Let us accept our own responsibility for the future."

-John F. Kennedy

Being A JFK Democrat

You may wonder why I am a JFK Democrat instead of a conservative Republican? The fact is that neither party is perfect for me. I am for business but not for unbridled corporate power. I am for unions but not for thug tactics in the workplace and I am not for forced unionism.

I worked for IBM for 23 years and at the time, IBM never had nor needed a union. Corporations should treat employees right and unions should be for the employees and not on the same team as the managers. At IBM, the founders believed that if you take care of the people, the people will take care of the business. It worked!

I am pro-life and I am against selling baby parts and live brains, though some legislators such as Bob Casey Jr. the incumbent, seems to have forgotten this. Deep down most Americans are pro-life. Who wants to kill babies when they are the most vulnerable--when they have not made their first goo or gaw?

I do not believe in protecting smelts and trees if it causes harm to human beings. God made human beings with dominion over all life, and though we must be just caretakers of this awesome responsibility, it should not mean that humans must starve or be cold or freeze in the wintertime to please somebody's twisted agenda.

In many ways some of the great ambitions of the Democratic Party leaders to create an equal world where there is no injustice has placed human beings per se in the back seat and has elevated non-humans to a status not intended by God. What good is it to freeze in the winter simply because the EPA has chosen to ban coal? I grew up with a coal stove in my living room and kitchen as did my wife, and we are still healthy. Plus, we (the USA) have plenty of coal for the rest of the world. Why shut off the spigot? Why? It makes no sense. China is killing us economically using coal!

Don't you think that protecting unborn babies is more important than protecting turtle eggs? Since it is a crime to destroy turtle eggs, at a minimum, it should also be a crime to kill an unborn child? Who is not pro baby? I think the big shot elite leaders of the Democratic Party have begun to endorse philosophies that give Government, rather than God, supreme power. I believe that God rules supreme above all else. When was the last time you were at a deathbed and heard the grieving family praying to the government?

Though recently I have come to like the philosophies of populists and conservatives like Marco Rubio and Donald Trump and Ben Carson and Ted Cruz. I am not for communists such as Bernie Sanders nor for wannabe communists such as Hillary Clinton. There is no good choice on the Democrat side. Sorry! JFK is sorely needed!

Like the Republican nominees, I do not think that corporations were meant to dominate individuals. I also think that American corporations have an obligation in exchange for the privilege of operating in America to care for their employees and to help do everything in their power to protect and create American Jobs.

Hiring illegal aliens must be verboten!

Republicans and many rich Democrats even prominent Democrats such as John Kerry and the Heinz Company have no problem taking jobs overseas. Additionally, they have no problem trying to reduce the American wage to as low as possible by bringing in illegal foreign workers to force the wages down.

Neither party wants to enforce our immigration laws. Republicans want lower wages and Democrats see a huge voter pool in those who are granted amnesty. I am for safe and secure borders and I believe in an America for Americans. If foreigners can live legally within our borders according to our laws, I am for that also. But, American citizens, that's us folks, must come first instead of last.

I would like to share with you information on a site that describes how to be a conservative (JFK) Democrat. My philosophies for the most part fit this description. http://www.ehow.com/how_2090667_be-conservative-democrat.html

How to Be a Conservative Democrat
Contributor: By eHow Contributing Writer
Article Rating: (11 Ratings)

In politics sometimes, it seems easy to categorize a person by their party affiliation. A Republican is conservative, and a Democrat is liberal. That is too limiting and shortsighted. Party affiliation does not eliminate individual thought. Defying these stereotypes is not always easy but is what democracy is based on--freedom of thought and choice.

Instructions for being a conservative Democrat

1. Step 1
Believe in small government. Small government means limiting the sprawling bureaucracy that invades people's lives and tries to tell them how to live those lives. Small government also means limiting monetary waste in government that comes with oversized government programs.

2. Step 2
Understand that there are services that the government needs to offer. While the conservative Democrat is against big government, they realize that some social programs are necessary for the country to thrive.

3. Step 3
Realize that a strong military force is a good. While curtailing government spending is prudent, it should not be at the expense of the nation's military. Even in times of peace, a strong military can be a deterrent to other aggressive countries and governments.

4. Step 4
Sympathize with the working class. A conservative democrat understands that the working class is the backbone that built this country. Conservative Democrats keep this in mind whenever taking issue with a policy or ideology.

5. Step 5
Focus on education and family values. Education and family values are an important part of the core values of the conservative Democrat. Education is what made this country a world leader and needs to be the focus of a conservative Democrats political agenda.

6. Step 6
Consider free market capitalism a positive endeavor. A conservative Democrat understands that the free market and capitalism empower the individual to make her own destiny.

For Democrats who feel as I do about life, I am clearly your candidate for Pennsylvania, and I would appreciate your vote.

Chapter 9 Mr. Smith Goes to Washington

Mr. Smith Goes to Washington

Ladies and Gentlemen, I would like to present myself. My name is Jefferson Smith and I am going to Washington—if you select me of course.

Jimmy Stewart is one of my favorite actors of all time. He is as Americana as it gets with the perfect touch of honesty that makes even men admire the actor and the character the actor is playing. My favorite movie of all time is "It's A Wonderful Life." It gets me every time. Remember the big pot of cash the neighbors brought in to George Bailey, so he could keep the Building and Loan going. Well, that's how I think America should be. Every hard-working American deserves a break.

What George Bailey did not need was the government stealing from his neighbors so that he could go to college and to heck with Pottersville. Well, it would have been Pottersville if George had not stayed to help all the people in Bedford Falls with his dad's Building and Loan Company. Government intervention creates Pottersvilles and good neighbors create the likes of Bedford Falls. Let's let good people be good people again rather than taking so much from them that Mr. Potter is the only one left with any money.

Mr. Smith Goes to Washington exudes the same emotion from the viewer. It was another of Frank Capra's big hits and Jimmy Stewart as Jefferson Smith is as down to earth as George Bailey. I don't propose that I can do as good a job for Northeastern PA as Jefferson Smith did for his constituency. However, I am as much a babe in the woods as far as politics go as Mr. Smith.

I am running for office to help fight the same type of corruption that Smith faced when he went to Washington. I am up to the task and I am ready to fight to make America, America again. There is nothing separating me from my chance other than this general election and your write-in. I thank you very much in advance for the vote.

You may know that Kelly is the second most common family name in Ireland (after Murphy). It is the 69th most popular surname in the United States. Kelly in many ways is like Jones and Smith.

And so, will you indulge me please as I say again. My name is Mr. Smith, and I am going to Washington. I can't get there without your help.

Think of the corrupt conditions that existed in this famous movie as Mr. Smith, played by Jimmy Stewart. Smith was little more than a bumpkin, when he first went into the Washington swamp of iniquity. For Smith, it was the US Senate. He was the naive and idealistic Jefferson Smith, the leader of the Boy Rangers. In Washington, Smith soon discovers many of the shortcomings of the political process as his earnest goal of a national boys' camp leads to a conflict with the state's corrupt political boss, Jim Taylor.

Taylor first tries to corrupt Smith and then later attempts to destroy Smith through a made-up scandal. Smith conducts a filibuster and finally sways everybody to not pass the healthcare bill. Wouldn't that be nice! (It was the Boy Rangers Bill). Smith would be working to get the bill repealed if it were passed, and the movie would have taken a bit longer. Kelly will make the repeal of the 2700 page bill a priority and will replace it with an EMTALA-like bill in the neighborhood of 4 to 8 pages. Additionally, Brian has a great plan for illegal interlopers and he will wipe out all student debt now and Boost Social Security so that the elderly can keep living in their homesteads.

Stranger things have happened. I hope to be like your Mr. Smith if you select me. And, so, I ask you to send me to Washington to serve in the United States Senate instead of Bob Casey. I hope there are approximately 32 additional like-thinking Senators sworn in when I have the honor to take office in January 2019. I want to thank you all. Thank you very much.

Chapter 10 Congress Needs to Be Sent Packing Today!

"Send the bums home. They need to get a job."
Sen. Rand Paul on term limits

If we ship them home, our pain is over!

My Name is Brian Kelly. I am not the coach of Notre Dame. I am from Northeastern Pennsylvania and I am running for the US Senate as a write-in candidate to help return government to the people.

I support the idea of an eight-point fix for both houses of Congress. It is enumerated at the end of this chapter.

There are a lot more problems than the solutions that it would take to solve them. For the most part, the solutions involve sending our self-centered greedy Senators, including Bob Casey Jr. packing out of Washington as fast as we can get them all the transportation. That alone would solve mostly everything that is wrong.

Representing the people is not and never was intended by our founders to be a career. The current system creates politicians from ordinary people when they choose to be in Congress for life representing their careers instead of the people.

If I gain the favor of the people in the 2018 general election, one of my first acts in the US Senate will be to sponsor a bill that has some good language or very similar language to get us back on track.

Remember this key point: Fixing Congress starts at home! Bob Casey in Pennsylvania is not immune to the people's needed fix. In fact, he is a major example of the problem. Members of Congress from both parties after two six-year terms should immediately be sent home. It starts right here in Pennsylvania if we have the guts.

I am a Democrat. My father was a Democrat. The Democratic Party that we see today is not our father's Democratic Party. It is not even for regular Americans. As a democrat myself, I know that we must clean out our Party of the elements that are blatantly trying to destroy our great country.

In 2016, I saw lifelong Democrats switching to the Republican Party just, so they could vote for Donald Trump and get away from the fringe-loving Democratic Party of today. If you are a regular hard-working American, the Democrats of today have no room for you at their table.

Today's Democratic Party led by Chuck Schumer and Nancy Pelosi, backed by almost 100% of the Democrats in Congress have enacted policies to kill America and especially regular Americans, especially white Americans. For some reason, all whites today are either racists or white supremacists, but I buy none of that.

Good people who love America must take over the Democratic Party and the people have to stop paying their money to see MSNBC, CBS, NBC, CNN, or any other anti-American Media Post. Cancel your NY Times subscription and you will hear more truth in your spare time.

A good number of Republicans who love lobbyists and donors and who have disdain for the rest of regular America should be voted out also, but they are not as bad as our Party. Democrats are single-handedly destroying everything that has made this nation great.

It is OK for Democrats to be values-oriented and have conservative principles. When anything goes, you get anything and the anything you get is typically not too good. A group called young conservatives has put together a simple and understandable list of nine different ways the Democrat Party has managed to ruin America.

I regret to say that Bob Casey who sites in the US Senate on behalf of PA Taxpayers is a disciple of this nine-point philosophy and must be replaced. Casey has proven that he is not one of us. Now that it is the election season again, if you watch closely, you might even catch a glimpse of his eminence in Pennsylvania if he has the time. They say every now and then that he sneaks out of his secure gated community to get a latte'.

Here are the nine points killing America. These are backed by Democrats in Congress and at all levels of the bureaucracy. Ask Bob Casey if he is the author of this list. Ask him why he and Maxine Watters want ICE eliminated?

1. Let criminals out
2. Let illegals in
3. Let boys in girl's locker rooms
4. Let women kill their offspring
5. Prosecute innocent police officers
6. Persecute Christians
7. Accept barbarity in the form of Islam
8. Over tax the hard working
9. Coddle the lazy

That just about does it. Bob Casey Jr has many extreme philosophies. They are well documented. You won't believe how radical Casey and many Democrats are since they have stopped being around the public.

Some things are eternal. I received this email on March 6, 2010. It still applies

From: "Friend" <friend@msnx.com>
To: "Brian Kelly" <campaign@briankellyforcongress.com>
Subject: Fw: Fw: Fwd: THIS IS HOW YOU FIX CONGRESS -
Date: Sat, 6 Mar 2010 11:17:41 -0500

X-Mailer: MSN 9
Seal-Send-Time: Sat, 6 Mar 2010 11:17:41 -0500
X-OriginalArrivalTime: 06 Mar 2010 16:17:48.0748 (UTC)
FILETIME=[902A80C0:01CABD48]

This is an email that is about ten years old.

THIS IS HOW YOU FIX CONGRESS!!!!!

In the meantime, of course, we must send them home. This notion
needs to be an amendment, not just an Act of Congress, just so they
can't change it again.

I have copied, pasted and sent this email to virtually everybody on my
e-mail list and that includes conservatives, liberals, and everybody in
between. Even though we disagree on a number of issues, I count all of
you who received this email as friends. The proposal is to promote a
"Congressional Reform Act of 2009." It would contain eight
provisions, all of which would probably be strongly endorsed by those
who drafted the Constitution and the Bill of Rights.

I know many of you will say, "This is impossible." Let me remind you
that Congress has the lowest approval of any entity in Government.
Now (At the time it was 2010 but still applies) is the time when
Americans must join together to reform Congress - the entity that
represents us or the representatives we elect will overrun us with their
assumed power.

We need to get a Senator to introduce this bill in the US Senate and a
Representative to introduce a similar bill in the US House. These
people will become American heroes. Please add any ideas on how to
get this done. Would any member of Congress give up their worldly
life to help their constituents? Ask Bob Casey Jr. his thoughts to get a
feel for whether the people can ever count on this greedy politician to
help their neighbors? You can count on me when you elect me to the
US Senate in 2018.

Thanks,
A Fellow American (with editing)

****

Congressional Reform Act of 2017

The Eight Point Fix for Congress

1. Term Limits: 12 years only, one of the possible options below.
A. Two Six-year Senate terms
B. Six Two-year House terms
C. One Six-year Senate term and three Two-Year House terms

Serving in Congress is an honor, not a career. The Founding Fathers envisioned citizen legislators. Serve your term(s), then go home and back to work.

2. No Tenure / No Pension:
A congressman collects a salary while in office and receives no pay (no retirement) when they are out of office. Serving in Congress is an honor, not a career. The Founding Fathers envisioned citizen legislators, serve your term(s), then go home and back to work.

3. Congress (past, present & future) participates in Social Security: All funds in the Congressional retirement fund moves to the Social Security system immediately. All future funds flow into the Social Security system, Congress participates with the American people. Serving in Congress is an honor, not a career. The Founding Fathers envisioned citizen legislators, server their short term(s), then going home and back to work.

4. Congress can purchase their own retirement plan just as all Americans. Serving in Congress is an honor, not a career. The Founding Fathers envisioned citizen legislators, serve your term(s), then go home and back to work.

5. Congress will no longer be allowed to vote themselves an "automatic" pay raise. Congressional pay will rise ONLY by the approval (vote) of the people they represent. Serving in Congress is an honor, not a career. The Founding Fathers envisioned citizen legislators, serve your term(s), then go home and back to work.

6. Congress loses its current health care system and participates in the same health care system as the American people. If it must be Obamacare, a system Congress enacted, so be it! Serving in Congress is an honor, not a career. The Founding Fathers envisioned citizen legislators, serve your term(s), then go home and back to work.

7. Congress must equally abide in all laws they impose on the American people.
Serving in Congress is an honor, not a career. The Founding Fathers envisioned citizen legislators, serve your term(s), then go home and back to work.

8. All contracts with past and present congressmen are void effective 1/1/17. The American people did not make this contract with congressmen, congressmen made all these contracts for themselves.

Serving in Congress is an honor, not a career. The Founding Fathers envisioned citizen legislators, serve your term(s), then go home and back to work.

Chapter 11 What happened to the Democratic Party?

Norman Mattoon Thomas
(November 20, 1884 - December 19, 1968)
was a leading American socialist, pacifist,
and six-time presidential candidate for the
Socialist Party of America.

The Socialist Party candidate for President
of the US, Norman Thomas, said this in a
1944 speech:

The American people will never knowingly adopt socialism.
But, under the name of 'liberalism,' they will adopt every fragment of
the socialist program, until one day America will be a socialist nation,
without knowing how it happened.'
He went on to say: 'I no longer need to run as a Presidential Candidate
for the Socialist Party.
The Democrat Party has adopted our platform.

An essay by Brian Kelly

Something happened to the Democratic Party since I first joined.
Before my dad passed away, we both noticed the big change. The
change was not good. It moved the party into being more and more
socialist. In many ways, it was so far left that it left the liberals far
behind in the rear-view mirror.

My father, though never a rich man, loved the American dream. He
loved what was his and envied nobody. As part of those who believe in
the dream, my dad believed deeply that we should all work hard, get
the best wage that we can, and we should be able to keep what we

earn. As a Brewery worker, my dad thought much like other hard laborers in Northeastern Pennsylvania, and that included the miners.

A number of my uncles earned their living from 5 AM to 5 PM in the coal mines, often never seeing the light of day in the short daylight of winter. The miners, the brewery workers, the coal men, and other factory workers in Northeastern PA were rugged individualists. They all loved freedom and they worked hard to enjoy the small breaks in the action. Their love of freedom and family helped them get up every day to put in that long day's work. And I can attest there are family members that even under such seemingly circumstances managed to be overweight. But, it just wasn't so bad!

Work is good for the heart

My career was not as tough as what these men had to put up with in their highly physical jobs. Unions were what helped them all even the score with management so that their wages were higher than mere subsistence. I did benefit from my dad's notion of work. As a very young boy, he picked coal along the railroad tracks to assure there was something to heat the family home. I had a similar youth experience.

When I was five years old, I am not joking when I say that my first job was as an entrepreneur. I used an old Radio Flyer Wagon or an old wheel barrow or a well-used baby carriage to collect papers and rags from my "customers" every Saturday. I worked within a five-block radius and I would knock on doors or ring the doorbells of my "customers." to pick up their old newspapers. I would take them to the junkyard that was less than two blocks from my house. I made about a quarter to thirty-five cents a week. It gave me an understanding of what it takes to work, and it put something in my pocket. It was a great life lesson.

I later moved on to shoveling sidewalks, cutting grass, working in a 5 & 10 (Huntzinger's 5 & 10), and then I spent time spotting pins in a bowling alley (WB Republics Club). I finished my high school career working on a soda truck (Eagle Bottling Works -- Zep-Up) and I inherited my older brother's paper route, which I turned over to my younger brother Joe when I graduated from Meyers High School in 1965.

At King's I was fortunate enough to get a work-study job in the maintenance department, and as I was scraping gum from the bottom of the tables in the library one day, I was invited to join the student aide's in the Computing Center. That was my first white collar job. One summer before I graduated, I had the pleasure of doing the payroll for the sellers and the cashiers at Pocono Downs, another white-collar job. After King's I began my career with IBM, which was most challenging and exciting.

I tell you all this because I hope to give you the right picture. I was doing manual labor from the time I was five years-old plus, though nothing like the miners of yesteryear, and I always had a blue-collar job or a clerical job or I had no money. It was that simple. My father taught me of the value of unions for the working man but when I joined IBM, there were no unions. All I had to do was my job and when I did it extremely well at IBM, I was rewarded with more than I had ever dreamed of in high school or in College.

Working for IBM was an experience of a lifetime. I have not stopped working but times have changed for me. I am ready to take on the challenge of representation for the people of Northeastern PA. I am a Democrat, but I am a traditional Democrat like my father, not one who longs for the day when an America of the future is ruled by communists.

One of the big differentiation factors between me and the Democratic Party Leaders is that I believe that if you work hard, you should keep what you earn. You should not be obligated to pay the freight for someone whose only problem in life is that they do not want to work.

In our democracy, in our freedom, in our American dream, those who are able to amass a huge bounty and those who are able to earn even a meager living do have obligations to the poor and the sick and those struggling with life. Even though we are morally obligated to try to help the helpless, income re-distribution by government is not the way.

Another objective of a country is to create a set of rugged individuals like our parents and grandparents that are prepared to help keep America strong. Yes, I am for helpless people, but I am not for making people helpless.

Having watched the Democratic Party evolve from the party of Harry Truman and Henry Scoop Jackson when I joined the party in the early 1970's, to the party of Chuck Schumer and Nancy Pelosi and quite frankly, like many of you, it makes me sick. The party has lost its moral underpinnings and basic understanding of its roots.

In the past, my party, the Democrats, were not afraid to defend and promote the freedom and rights of every American. Now in what I would have to call a contaminated state, they support the abandonment of the Constitution; the power of the government to force an unwanted and unpopular health care system on the American populace; the diminution of black Americans through abortion; money laundering of taxpayer funds through unions and using documented Saul Alinsky strategies to demonize their opposition with the help of a one-sided corrupt press.

Is it Democrats or their leadership or both? I wonder. I know who I am, but I do not claim to know all Democrats. I am a Democrat, but I do not think like the new fringe-loving Democrat Party. I ask myself for example, why would Democrats seem to love Al Sharpton? I am white and Irish. Sharpton does not make comments about the Irish but he is always chipping at the dignity of white people in America.

Mr. Sharpton is anti-white, anti-Semite, a liar, a con man, and a hustler who extorts millions from corporations. On top of that he is a habitual tax cheat with continual White House visitation privileges during the "O" years. Al owes millions to the IRS, but they have given the Reverend a pass. Yet he keeps appearing as the face of the Democratic Party. Is it so? Is Al Sharpton, white or black, all we Democrats have in our foot locker? What is the Democratic Party? Maybe it is not worth talking about? Maybe it is just in need of resuscitation?

Chapter 12 Americans Are in Revolt.

Countervailing power is the only solution!

Those with power sometimes do not know how powerful they are
while those without power know very well how weak they are. The
have's always have and the have-nots, have not ever--but they do their
best to survive. So, it has been from the beginning of time as the major
law of the universe dictates: "survival of the fittest."

Are humans above it all? Is there just a little bit in a human that is
animal? Is it possible that part really is not as good in its spirit as man's
best friend, the wonderful creature called dog? Are humans or dogs
more inclined to do the right thing if called upon accordingly? Tough
question!

I look into my wonderful dog's eyes and I know which way he is going
to go. When I look a human in the eye, it is my history with the person
more than the look in his eye that matters. But, the look in his eye does
matter. I admit that it is good to have a fine canine friend help out in
the evaluation. Who is good; and who is bad? Dogs seem to know!

As we go back to the turn of the 20th century we find certain humans who had lots and lots of material goods as well as lots of power. These folks were truly captains of industry and they were referred to as "Robber Barons." That term was not very flattering to these people who went to church each week in fine clothes, hoping to charm even the priests into believing in their goodness. But, there was little goodness there!

Robber Barons was not a very flattering term for anybody at the time and it is not a well-appreciated term today. It implies that certain Barons are robbers. They rob the people. We all know who they are and who they were in real times from our unedited American History classes. John D. Rockefeller, Milton S. Hershey, J.P. Morgan, Andrew Carnegie, and Cornelius Vanderbilt were the headliner robber barons of the period. They were all shrewd, cunning, and some might add heartless businessmen of the period. Even they may not have known they were so bad. .

These Robber Barons were indeed captains of industry and they were indeed, robber barons.

They had immense power and ran huge companies and hired many people to work in their facilities. For the workers, it was good because they had a job and they were able to provide for their families, though just barely. For the families, it was not so good because the head of the household had to work most of his waking hours every day of the week. The Robber Barons believed, perhaps even sincerely, that they were providing a modicum of wealth for the plebeians of the new America.

There is a very offensive term that has been used for some time to describe one of the worst acts of the Robber Barons. This term is "labor arbitrage." It came from this period of American History as the Robber Barons tried their best to assure that the wage they paid was the absolute minimal wage. And, they did pay only as much as legally required.

Only the Robber Barons held the power in the period before and immediately after the turn of the twentieth century. The irony is that the workers did not really understand their value in the wealth creation process. The workers were the means to the Barons' wealth. Yet, they had no power, and in most cases were living in destitute circumstances.

The worker had power but could not realize it individually. This enabled the barons to exact upon the workers whatever terms were favorable to the barons alone. The workers were mere resources. Though they were clearly the means to the barons' wealth, nobody on the Robber Baron team was about to reveal this to them.

In the power game, the barons had all the power and the workers had none. -- zero, nada, zilch as they like to say today. Thus, there was a power void. Whenever there is a power void, it will eventually be filled as the seemingly powerless realize that in numbers, they have power. In the days of the Robber Barons, the barons were able to essentially enslave the workers because there was no notion of a countervailing power, and no means of achieving it even if the notion were well known.

What is countervailing power and why is it important?

Wikipedia authors often get it right, "Modern economies give massive powers to large business corporations to bias this process, and there arise 'countervailing' powers in the form of trade unions, citizens' organizations and so on, to offset business's excessive advantage."

Corporations at the turn of the century were just becoming legal and powerful and this was coincident with the Robber Baron period. Corporations were like little dictatorships that created worker cities ruled mostly by tyrants all within the democracy of the United States. This was not a proud moment in American History.

The greed exhibited by one corporation during this period forced another corporation to be as greedy as the first or go out of business. So, corporations and the men (at the time) who ran them, chose to be as greedy as they could be. They viewed it as much a matter of survival as a means to success.

The conditions were perfect. There was a large supply of labor and many needy families willing to send any member into the factory. This set the stage for the ultimate labor arbitrage. So, let's examine this notion of labor arbitrage in light of countervailing power. Quite simply, Labor arbitrage is the movement of the wage which industry must pay for workers to the lowest possible level.

Labor arbitrage creates big hurts in lots of regular people. In many ways in 2018, the "new immigrants," undocumented workers," "illegal foreign nationals," or quite simply, "illegal aliens, are driving American wages down again to the point of labor arbitrage, and it is not by accident.

The Robber Barons are documented as having exploited Americans, using sweatshops with abysmally low wages. They were fully in control of the labor arbitrage. If workers had to work just 10 hours a day, it was an easy shop but sometimes the periods included 18-hour work shifts, without overtime pay. The abuses of the period included child labor; inadequate safety, minimal health and environmental safeguards; and of course, no pension or health benefits--for most Americans.

There seemed to be no escape. If a worker of that era tried to change his plight, he might be summarily discharged for union organizing. There were a lot of reasons for families to just accept their condition as it was dealt. The Robber Barons assured that those who accepted their dire circumstances were able to survive, though in the most meager ways.

Humans are animals and when animals are pinched and hurt, and their young are hurting, life is different than when you and I are screaming at the TV set because of things as trite as that our favorite team did not score. If the team is Notre Dame, and if I (Brian Kelly) were the coach, then perhaps the screaming would be appropriate and responsible. But, that again is not the theme of this chapter.

Eventually, when you are really hurting, finding a solution because of the gravity of a problem such as labor arbitrage with no countervailing power is far more important than the fear of repercussions. A solution must come one way or another. From every void a solution will come.

At the turn of the last century, however, there was a huge void. People were hurting, and it seemed they were helpless. However, every now and then, brave men would come by to help. These were union organizers and they tried their best to fill the void. The union organizers intrinsically knew that giving power to the worker was the only solution to labor arbitrage.

Yet, employees knew that the best they could do would be to be able to barely make it if they made no waves at all. If they made some waves, such as fraternizing with a labor organizer, they might be left with nothing. The choice to organize was difficult as the risks were high.

The union workers were very brave souls with a real mission. They suffered, and all suffered when trying to take the smallest action to avoid the tyranny of the Robber Barons. Can you imagine working for the Baron and trying to overcome the Baron at the same time?

There is an idea that if a decent wage were paid to the workers-- not substantially larger but seemingly generous, the Robber Barons would have been able to keep their gold and the worker would have achieved the opportunity to live more hours per week with family, rather than at the factory. But, with no countervailing power, the Robber Barons were more concerned about competing against other Robber Barons. They had no regard at all for the power of the worker who was merely part of the means of production. The worker simply had no power.

Wherever and whenever there is a power void, it will be filled.

Over time, unions developed strategies to face and to compete against the all-powerful captains of industry, the Robber Barons. They demanded better wages and better benefits for workers. The unions became the countervailing power against the Robber Barons / corporations that had been missing from the foray for far too long.

Soon after unions were integrated into the fabric of America, life got better for everybody -- workers and even the former barons. Though the sins of the Robber Barons were hard to forgive, the unions helped them to stop sinning against their fellow human-kind.

Enter the Politician

Political corruption is not new to our times. When the Robber Barons had the wealth, there were plenty of politicians who favored their way of life and benefited from it immensely. The people did not count. The political process has not changed much, unfortunately.

When the unions gained power, and perhaps as a means of that power, there were politicians who recognized the winds of change and prepared to accept their largesse from Unions as there had come a choice.

Once the countervailing power had been duly established, neither corporations nor unions controlled the scenario. Both were very powerful, and the unions did their best for the worker while the corporation did its best for the former baron class citizens.

Eventually both the corporations and the unions noticed that there was a very large and available third party that had entered the ring. Actually, it had always been there but in the early days it represented only we the people. The third party was actually to have been the "people" as represented by the Congress, the Senate, the President, and the Supreme Court. Instead, the third party in its public face was just the government with all of its inelegant bureaucracy.

Of course, when it chose to do so, and only when it was inclined, this third party known as the government, did claim to represent ordinary people. However, most of the time, as we have all come to realize in 2018, the temptation of the politician to feed himself from the public troth is so overwhelming that he has little time to include we the people in his greed-driven thought process. Self-serving politicians are more visible today because they promise the people everything to get elected.

John Quinton called it right when he described the greed of a politician in this way: "Politicians are people who, when they see light at the end of the tunnel, go out and buy some more tunnel."

The corporations and the unions fought for the control of this powerful entity known as the government. Whoever won over the politician had the tie breaker on their side. For the most part, only at election time did the people matter. And, we know politicians love their perquisites. Depending on which politician was on-the-take or as they would like to have it said, "depending on which group got the politician's ear," things moved in that direction with a little help from government friends.

Does that sound like today? Does that sound like Bob Casey's US Senate? Why did Bob Casey Jr. not vote to reduce the tax burden on Americans? He'll tell you that Nancy Pelosi and Chuck Schumer told him to vote against putting more in Americans' pockets because the crumbs were not worth it. Yet, today's Americans have grown accustomed to the thousands of dollars in "crumbs" they otherwise would never have been able to spend.

None of my Democrat friends want to give back two or three thousand a year or more to the government? Remember this. Bob Casey Jr. thinks that you do. He thinks you do not need extra money. Brian Kelly thinks you enjoy every dime you get to spend even if someone else calls them crumbs. Elect Bob Casey and the crumbs and the thousands of dollars will go away. Elect Brian Kelly and the thousands you have will multiply and the rest of the country will also prosper.

God bless you all.

One Last Thought!

There is some good news. People are beginning to think that things are out of control and perhaps the countervailing power will have to be some type of internal revolt that helps even things out again.

Mark Thoma had some time on Tuesday, May 15, 2012 at 12:15 AM while sitting in an airline seat and so he posted this great little perspective piece in Economics, Fiscal Policy, and Politics. I have included this short post below and several appropriate comments. He titled his piece as follows:

Tuesday, May 15, 2012

The Need for Countervailing Power

http://economistsview.typepad.com/economistsview/2012/05/the-need-for-countervailing-power.html

(Though it won't post until later, I may as well try to do something while I sit in this airplane seat.)

Like Brad DeLong, before the recession started I could not have imagined that policymakers would fail to put the unemployed first and foremost in all policy decisions. I was sure the unemployed would come before inflation, before banks, before debt reduction and contrived fights over the debt ceiling. How could we possibly turn our backs on millions of struggling households, especially when doing so creates so many additional long-run problems for individual households and for the economy as a whole? Nothing else would be more important than putting people back to work, and we would, of course, come together and mobilize in a national war against high unemployment.

But I forgot something. With the decline in unions in recent decades, the working class has lost both economic and political power. And at the same time, those at the top end of the income scale have gained power both relatively and absolutely. So why would I have ever thought that the unemployed would come first when they have so little organized political power? Is it any surprise that policy has paid most attention to the issues that just happen to be the things those with the most political power care the most about? What was I thinking?

I suppose I was thinking that politicians were honorable, that money wouldn't trump principle. Silly me. In any case, the question is how to change the balance of power. We could get the money out of politics, but that will never be fully possible. Even with the best of effort, loopholes, bypasses, and the like will always be sought out, found, and exploited too circumvent the rules. That doesn't mean we shouldn't try -- whatever constraints can be imposed are helpful -- but this probably isn't the full answer. We could hope for better politicians, people who represent everyone equally, including the powerless, but I'm certainly not going to count on that either. Finally, we could try to provide (or at least not discourage) a countervailing force, something that replaces the role that unions played for the working class.

I'm not completely sure what form this institution should take, workers lack both economic power in wage negotiations and political power to shape legislation in their favor, or how it could happen short of fed up workers finally demanding change. But workers need to have their interests better represented, and the need for a new institution of some sort is clear.

Comments:

dilbert dogbert said in reply to reason...
When union members are unemployed the union will advocate for them. The union will of course focus its efforts on union members first and foremost. Just like CEO's focus first and foremost on their bonuses.

Min said in reply ...
"The best explanation for this that I can see is that Capital and the bourgeoisie has globalized while the proletariat remains fundamentally national."
Workers of the world, unite!

christy said...
What is needed is a "consumer union".
A consumer union could exercise power by refusing to buy the goods and services of corporations in certain limited circumstances.
Furthermore, the union could gain members by exercising market power and negotiating price reductions for members.

Such a union could be very effective as against, for example, pharmaceutical companies that abuse the patent system by encouraging members to buy competing products across that companies' entire product range.
Modern social media would make the organization of such a union very easy indeed.

And all that would be required form members would be a willingness to refrain from buying certain products when requested.
If well-organized such an organization could be effective - its market power would also benefit from network effects and increasing returns form scale

---

And, so, it is what it is! Remember that a write-in vote is an exercise in countervailing power.

Other Books by Brian Kelly: (amazon.com, and Kindle)

It's Time for The John Doe Party… Don't you think? By By Elephants.
Great Players in Florida Gators Football… Tim Tebow and a ton of other great players
Great Coaches in Florida Gators Football… The best coaches in Gator history.
The Constitution by Hamilton, Jefferson, Madison, et al. The Real Constitution
The Constitution Companion. Will help you learn and understand the Constitution
Great Coaches in Clemson Football The best Clemson Coaches right to Dabo Sinney
Great Players in Clemson Football The best Clemson players in history
Winning Back America. America's been stolen and can be won back completely
The Founding of America… Great book to pick up a lot of great facts
Defeating America's Career Politicians. The scoundrels need to go.
Midnight Mass by Jack Lammers… You remember what it was like Hreat story
The Bike by Jack Lammers… Great heartwarming Story by Jack
Wipe Out All Student Loan Debt--Now! Watch the economy go boom!
No Free Lunch Pay Back Welfare! Why not pay it back?
Deport All Millennials Now!!! Why they deserve to be deported and/or saved
DELETE the EPA, Please! The worst decisions to hurt America
Taxation Without Representation 4th Edition Should we throw the TEA overboard again?
Four Great Political Essays by Thomas Dawson
Top Ten Political Books for 2018… Cliffnotes Version of 10 Political Books
Top Six Patriotic Books for 2018… Cliffnotes version of 6 Patriotic Boosk
Why Trump Got Elected!.. It's great to hear about a great milestone in America!
The Day the Free Press Died. Corrupt Press Lives on!
Solved (Immigration) The best solutions for 2018
Solved II (Obamacare, Social Security, Student Debt) Check it out; They're solved.
Great Moments in Pittsburgh Steelers Football... Six Super Bowls and more.
Great Players in Pittsburgh Steelers Football ,,,Chuck Noll, Bill Cowher, Mike Tomin, etc.
Great Coaches in New England Patriots Football,,, Bill Belichick the one and only plus others
Great Players in New England Patriots Football… Tom Brady, Drew Bledsoe et al.
Great Coaches in Philadelphia Eagles Football..Andy Reid, Doug Pederson & Lots more
Great Players in Philadelphia Eagles Football Great players such as Sonny Jurgenson
Great Coaches in Syracuse Football All the greats including Ben Schwartzwalder
Great Players in Syracuse Football. Highlights best players such as Jim Brown & Donovan McNabb
Millennials are People Too !!! Give US millennials help to live American Dream
Brian Kelly for the United States Senate from PA: Fresh Face for US Senate
The Candidate's Bible. Don't pray for your campaign without this bible
Rush Limbaugh's Platform for Americans… Rush will love it
Sean Hannity's Platform for Americans… Sean will love it
Donald Trump's New Platform for Americans. Make Trump unbeatable in 2020
Tariffs Are Good for America! One of the best tools a president can have
Great Coaches in Pittsburgh Steelers Football Sixteen of the best coaches ever to coach in pro football.
Great Moments in New England Patriots Football Great football moments from Boston to New England
Great Moments in Philadelphia Eagles Football. The best from the Eagles from the beginning of football.
Great Moments in Syracuse Football The great moments, coaches & players in Syracuse Football
Boost Social Security Now! Hey Buddy Can You Spare a Dime?
The Birth of American Football. From the first college game in 1869 to the last Super Bowl
Obamacare: A One-Line Repeal Congress must get this done.
A Wilkes-Barre Christmas Story A wonderful town makes Christmas all the better
A Boy, A Bike, A Train, and a Christmas Miracle A Christmas story that will melt your heart
Pay-to-Go America-First Immigration Fix
Legalizing Illegal Aliens Via Resident Visas Americans-first plan saves $Trillions. Learn how!
60 Million Illegal Aliens in America!!! A simple, America-first solution.
The Bill of Rights By Founder James Madison Refresh your knowledge of the specific rights for all
Great Players in Army Football Great Army Football played by great players..
Great Coaches in Army Football Army's coaches are all great.
Great Moments in Army Football Army Football at its best.
Great Moments in Florida Gators Football Gators Football from the start. This is the book.
Great Moments in Clemson Football CU Football at its best. This is the book.
Great Moments in Florida Gators Football Gators Football from the start. This is the book.
The Constitution Companion. A Guide to Reading and Comprehending the Constitution
The Constitution by Hamilton, Jefferson, & Madison – Big type and in English

PATERNO: The Dark Days After Win # 409. Sky began to fall within days of win # 409.
JoePa 409 Victories: Say No More! Winningest Division I-A football coach ever
American College Football: The Beginning From before day one football was played.
Great Coaches in Alabama Football Challenging the coaches of every other program!
Great Coaches in Penn State Football the Best Coaches in PSU's football program
Great Players in Penn State Football The best players in PSU's football program
Great Players in Notre Dame Football The best players in ND's football program
Great Coaches in Notre Dame Football The best coaches in any football program
Great Players in Alabama Football from Quarterbacks to offensive Linemen Greats!
Great Moments in Alabama Football AU Football from the start. This is the book.
Great Moments in Penn State Football PSU Football, start--games, coaches, players,
Great Moments in Notre Dame Football ND Football, start, games, coaches, players
Cross Country with the Parents A great trip from East Coast to West with the kids
Seniors, Social Security & the Minimum Wage. Things seniors need to know.
How to Write Your First Book and Publish It with CreateSpace
The US Immigration Fix--It's all in here. Finally, an answer.
I had a Dream IBM Could be #1 Again The title is self-explanatory
WineDiets.Com Presents The Wine Diet Learn how to lose weight while having fun.
Wilkes-Barre, PA; Return to Glory Wilkes-Barre City's return to glory
Geoffrey Parsons' Epoch... The Land of Fair Play Better than the original.
The Bill of Rights 4 Dummmies! This is the best book to learn about your rights.
Sol Bloom's Epoch ...Story of the Constitution The best book to learn the Constitution
America 4 Dummmies! All Americans should read to learn about this great country.
The Electoral College 4 Dummmies! How does it really work?
The All-Everything Machine Story about IBM's finest computer server.
ThankYou IBM! This book explains how IBM was beaten in the computer marketplace by neophytes

Brian has written 171 books in total. Other books can be found at amazon.com/author/brianwkelly

www.ingramcontent.com/pod-product-compliance
Lightning Source LLC
Chambersburg PA
CBHW060909280326
41934CB00007B/1246